PIT BOSS Wood Pellet Grill and Smoker Bible 2022

The Ultimate Cookbook with 1700 Days Super-Juicy BBQ Recipes to Release your Inner Caveman & Become the Undisputed Pitmaster Among your Friends

Cole Palmer

TABLE OF CONTENT

INTRODUCTION — 7
How do you use the Pit Boss pellet grill? — 7
How does the Pit Boss Grill work? — 7
Understand the ingredients of cooking — 8
Does Pit Boss have PID controllers? — 9

SWITCHING ON THE GRILL FOR THE FIRST TIME — 10
BEEF CUTS — 13
FISH CUTS — 14
LAMB CUTS — 15
PORK CUTS — 16
CHICKEN CUTS — 17

THE DIFFERENT TYPES OF SALT — 18

MARINADES — 19

BRINE — 21

RUB — 22

HOW TO PREPARE YOUR PIT ON — 26

BREAKFAST — 29
Smoked Cheesecake — 30
Smoked Peaches — 29
Baked Breakfast Sausage Casserole — 31
Baked Candied Bacon Cinnamon Rolls — 30
Breakfast Smoked Casserole — 32
Smoked Cheese and Bacon Egg Bites — 31
Smoked Tasty Breakfast Fatty — 33
Tasty Breakfast Grilled Pizza — 34

APPETIZERS — 35
Grilled Chicken Wings — 35
Grilled Filet Mignon — 39
Bacon-wrapped stuffed pickles — 36
Applewood bacon jalapeno poppers — 36
Smoked Rosemary and Blood Orange Spritz — 37
Grilled Cocktail with Melon — 37
Pig in a Hammock Cocktail — 38
Smoked Texas-Style Ranch Water — 38
Bubz and Smoke Cocktail — 39
Smoke and Beer Cocktail — 39

PORK RECIPES — 40
Raspberry Chipotle Flavored Pork Kebabs — 41
Asparagus Wrapped in Bacon — 43
Grilled Peppercorn Pork Chops — 40
Rosemary Grilled Pork Chops — 41
Raspberry Flavored Spiral Ham — 42
Cubano Pork Sandwiches — 42
Nachos with Pulled Pork — 43
Beer Braised Grilled Pork Belly — 44
Pork Chops Stuffed with Cheesy Potatoes — 44

KOREAN PULLED PORK 45

OVERNIGHT TAMARIND SPARE RIBS 46

PORK CHOPS WITH GRILLED MANGO PINEAPPLE SALSA 47

MEDITERRANEAN MEATBALLS IN SPICY TOMATO SAUCE 48

SMOKED PORK SAUSAGE WITH BISCUITS AND GRAVY 49

BEEF RECIPES 50

SMOKED ROAST BEEF 51

SMOKED BURGERS 51

SMOKED BEEF RIBS 51

PELLET GRILL MEATLOAF 52

BBQ BRISKET 53

TRI-TIP ROAST 53

FULLY LOADED BEEF NACHOS 54

ITALIAN MEATBALLS 54

SWEET & SOUR BRISKET 55

CHICKEN AND TURKEY RECIPES 56

CHICKEN BREASTS PELLET GRILL WITH FETA AND FRESH MINT 57

SALT-AND-PEPPER BONELESS CHICKEN 57

CHICKEN SATAY WITH THAI PEANUT SAUCE 58

CHICKEN SALAD WITH MANGO AND FRESH HERBS 59

SHEET PAN ROASTED CHICKEN 59

CHICKEN WITH ALABAMA SAUCE 60

ANCHO-CHILE SMOKED CHICKEN 62

BBQ CHICKEN THIGHS 62

CHICKEN ROAST WITH POTATOES 61

BACON WRAPPED CHICKEN 63

PRETZEL MUSTARD CHICKEN 63

BAKED PROSCIUTTO-WRAPPED CHICKEN BREAST WITH SPINACH AND BOURSIN 60

SEAFOOD RECIPES 64

SWEET HONEY SOY SMOKED SALMON 66

CRANBERRY LEMON SMOKED MACKEREL 67

CITRUSY SMOKED TUNA BELLY WITH SESAME AROMA 68

SAVORY SMOKED TROUT WITH FENNEL AND BLACK PEPPER RUB 69

SWEET SMOKED SHRIMPS GARLIC BUTTER 65

SPICED SMOKED CRABS WITH LEMON GRASS 70

TEQUILA ORANGE MARINADE SMOKED LOBSTER 72

GRILLED SALMON BURGER 73

GRILLED SWORDFISH 65

GRILLED FISH TACOS 74

MANDARIN SALMON 73

TUNA NOODLE CASSEROLE 7

SMOKED WHITE SALAD 7

LAMB RECIPES 75

SEASONED LAMB SHOULDER 76

LEMONY & SPICY LAMB SHOULDER 76

SWEET & TANGY BRAISED LAMB SHANK 77

WOOD PELLET SMOKED LAMB SHOULDER 77

WOOD PELLET SMOKED PULLED LAMB SLIDERS 78

WOOD PELLET SMOKED LEG OF LAMB 78

SIMPLE GRILLED LAMB CHOPS   79

BRAISED LAMB SHANK   79

LAMB CHOPS WITH ROSEMARY   80

IRISH LAMB STEW   81

ROASTED LAMB SHOULDER   82

GRILLED LAMB BURGER   83

GRILLED LAMB CHOPS   84

VEGGIE RECIPES   85

GRILLED CORN WITH HONEY AND BUTTER   85

GRILLED SWEET POTATO PLANKS   86

ROASTED VEGGIES AND HUMMUS   86

GRILLED SPICY SWEET POTATOES   86

GRILLED MEXICAN STREET CORN   87

PERFECTLY SMOKED ARTICHOKE HEARTS   87

GRILLED GREENS AND CHEESE QUESADILLAS   88

GRILLED CORN ON THE COB   88

WOOD PELLET SMOKED MUSHROOMS   87

DESSERTS   89

BROWNIE BREAD BAKED PUDDING   90

CHERRY CRISP LAYERED WITH SWEET CREAM   91

GRILLED WATERMELON AND PINEAPPLE CREAM SICLES   92

GINGERBREAD BAKED COOKIES   93

BUTTERMILK PIE BAKED WITH CORNMEAL CRUST   94

S'MORES SMOKED CAKE BARS   92

BACON BOURBON BROWNIES   95

CHERRY PIE SPICED   96

VEGAN PUMPKIN APPLE MUFFINS GLUTEN-FEE   97

SKILLET CHEESECAKE BROWNIE   97

CONCLUSION   98

100

INTRODUCTION

Wood pellet grills are now enjoying great popularity. Pit Boss Wood Pellet Grill is one of the best brands for people who want a quality grill without paying a high price. Regardless of whether you are thinking about buying a pellet grill or just want to learn how to use the Pit Boss pellet grill, you've come to the right place. I've had my own pit boss for a little over a year now, and here's what I've learned during that time.

HOW DO YOU USE THE PIT BOSS PELLET GRILL?

In the 1990s, Dan Thiessen came up with the idea of a pellet grill when his chimney company started converting wood waste into pellets. This concept led his family to become a pellet stove manufacturer. Anyone can cook indirectly with a wide variety of Pit Boss Pellets, making it easy to prepare delicious meals right in your yard.

Pellet grills are made of natural wood. After adding to the pellet funnel, the auger guides them into the pan, where they light up and cook food in the cooking zone.

In contrast to conventional grills, several Pit Boss models have a capacity of 8-1, making them the second most popular grill after the Traeger brand.

HOW DOES THE PIT BOSS GRILL WORK?

Let's explain the most important parts of a pellet grill, whatever brand you are.

Ignitor

The igniter is one of the problems with any pellet grill. The igniter is what ignites the pellets in the crucible. You can still start the grill if the igniter fails, but you will need to light the fire with a propane burner.

Induction fan

The first point you will notice when you turn on your Pit Boss grill is the noise level from the induction fan. The sound of a pellet motor is normal, especially when it is started.

The induction fan remains switched on during the entire cooking process. Hardwood smoke circulates through the cooking space, making it possible to cook in convection mode.

Auger

The auger is the big screw that drives the burner. You can control the pellet flow with the P setting on the control panel. A higher P-value causes the screw to stop for a longer period of time, which slows down the feeding of the pellets into the crucible.

It will take you a while to learn how to adjust the Pit Boss' P setting—continuing to use your grill will teach you how to use it, especially in cold weather.

Fire Pot

The pan contains the pellets and ash residues in the grill. When enough pellets are burning, the hot rod will ignite them. The induction fan then ignites the fire, creating the famous induction heat.

Hoper

It is a large storage container that is attached to the granulate shelf. The only job of the funnel is to take the pellets, which are brought into the cooking chamber by means of an endless screw.

Before starting Pit Boss, you need to make sure that there are enough pellets in the funnel for the entire cooking time.

UNDERSTAND THE INGREDIENTS OF COOKING

Similar to a charcoal and gas grill. Pellet grills contain certain cooking ingredients that make it easier to cook meat, vegetables, etc.

Top shelf

Most Pit Boss models have a removable top shelf. Think of the top shelf as an additional cooking space. For example, if you are making 18 hamburgers on the lower shelf and you run out of space, you can use the upper shelf for extra space.

Just keep in mind that food will take longer to cook on the top shelf because it is further away from the fire. Many people on online forums say they didn't notice the difference in cooking times when using the top shelf. However, it's always the best idea to use a thermometer while cooking in the pit boss. It's easier to make sure you're cooking meat to the correct core temperature.

Lower hob

The main cooking area consists of removable grill racks on which most food is cooked. It is located directly on the flame grill and makes toasting food easier.

The dimensions of the cooking zone can vary depending on the model. The stainless steel 2-burner gas grill has a cooking surface of 267.8 square inches. While the Pit Boss Series 7 vertical smoker has a cooking surface of 1,853 square inches.

No problem what type of model you have; the cooking space will be different. Before buying a pellet grill, make sure you have a grill that is big enough for your needs.

The flame grill makes grilling over a flame easier. Use the sliding plate to open the fire when grilling with a direct flame. This makes it easy to fry burgers, steaks, hot dogs, etc., which I've never seen before.

I first used it for the burgers that I cooked, and the flame just popped off the fiery grill. These were the tastiest burgers I've ever made, and I loved the scorch marks they left on the pies.

It's also handy when you're cooking in a cast iron pan.

This is how the Pit Boss temperature scale works.

Depending on the model, you have the following controls:
- Temperature
- On / Off button
- Setting P
- Meat probes
- LCD screen

On / Off button

Press the button to turn the grill device on / off. When linked to a power source, the power switch glows blue.

Temperature

The control panel shows both the set and the actual temperatures. This makes it easy to tell if your grill is hotter or colder than you should without lifting the lid.

Setting P

Use the rotary knob P on the control panel to set the auger operation.

Meat probes

There are two connections for connecting the temperature sensor. When the core temperature probe is connected, the internal temperature of the meat is displayed on the LCD screen.

LCD screen

The LCD screen shows the current cooking temperature, the desired cooking temperature and the temperature of the core probe.

DOES PIT BOSS HAVE PID CONTROLLERS?

At one point, Pit Boss didn't offer PID-controlled grills and smokehouse. All models worked on used time controls. Until recently, Pit Boss issued the Rauch IT control card.

Smoke IT temperature technology allows you to control the temperature of the grill with your phone via Bluetooth. I recently added a smoke IT checklist to my pit boss, and you can watch the video here.

SWITCHING ON THE GRILL FOR THE FIRST TIME

According to the Pit Boss book, the first time the grill is used, all you need to do is " turn the temperature knob/control to the highest temperature and let the grill run for 30-40 minutes with the lid closed." This will ensure that any foreign objects, debris, etc., are burned off before you cook for the first time.

Here is a video of how I refueled my pit boss after assembling it.

These are the steps I followed when starting up my Pit Boss Pro 820. These are the same steps that you can find in the instruction manual.

1. Check the funnel and remove any debris or debris.
2. Remove all cooking ingredients from the grill.
3. Connect the grill to a power source.
4. Turn on the grill device and turn the T control on smoking.
5. Open the hopper cover to make sure the auger is working properly.
6. Place your hand on the brazier to check the airflow.
7. After a minute, you will smell the detonator, and the air will get hotter. (Do not touch)
8. After making sure that all electrical components are working, turn off your grill.
9. Fill the funnel with all-natural wood pellets. (preferably Pit Boss brand)
10. Return the grill to the smoking position while holding the Prime button.
11. Hold the Prime button until the first pellets fall into the crucible.
12. Now turn on the grill at high power (500 ° F) and close the lid.
13. Let it run for 30-40 minutes.
14. Close the grate.
15. It's flavorful and ready to grill!

Procedure for shutting down the quarry

According to the Pit Boss book, the turn-off procedure allows the grill to go through a natural cleaning process. It removes excess fat from your last cooking session.

After you have taken the food off the grill, set the temperature control to the maximum value and let it cook for another 5-10 minutes with the lid closed. The burning process reduces the risk of fat burning the next time you turn on the grill.

Fireplace setting Pit Boss

The chimney affects the airflow inside the main grill. If you're cooking at a lower temperature, leave a wider opening on the lid.

It takes time to learn how to regulate a fireplace, and everyone is different. Some avid barbecues say they never regulate their chimney. Personally, I never touched my fireplace, except when cleaning it.

Can you use pellets in Pit Boss?

Pit Boss recommends using high-quality hardwood pellets. This means that you can use Traeger pellets or other high-quality pellets in your smokehouse. If you see a pellet with a different flavor that Pit Boss doesn't make, you can swap it out and use other brands of pellets.   Always use high-quality pellets. Poor quality pellets can affect the performance of your pellet grill.

How much time do the pellets last in the Pit Boss Grill?

In my personal experience, a 40-pound bag will last 12-40 hours on low or high heat. The shelf life of the pellets naturally depends on the quality of the pellets, the P setting, the temperature setting and the cooking time.

The lower the heat and the longer the cooking time, the more pellets you will burn.

Pit Boss Pellets can be purchased on pages 20 and 20 pounds.

What action should I take if my pit boss runs out of pellets while in use?

When you have it on hand, just open the lid and add something to the funnel.

However, if the grill is left unattended and you lose heat, you will need to turn the device grill off and let it cool completely before starting it again.

According to the Pit Boss book, it says that if it goes out, you will need to restart the boot process. However, I have found that this is only the case when the pellets are completely used up and no longer remain in the auger or crucible.

How do I heat up a Pit Boss pellet grill?

In contrast to conventional grills, pit boss grills are very easy to heat up.

To start heating the pit boss, press the power button and set the temperature controller to your desired temperature like in an oven.

If you've used a charcoal grill before, you know how difficult it is to get started. In contrast to gas and pellet grills, it does not contain starters or hoses. You will most likely need lighter fluid to light the fire, and maintaining the temperature can be difficult.

A gas grill can be more difficult to light, especially if it is an old grill and the igniter is worn out, or the grill has not been used for a long time. If the pilot runs out, you can still light him with a long bic lighter, but this is not always a safe option.

In comparison, pit boss grills are easy to ignite.

When you're almost ready to cook, just open the lid and press the power button. The temperature controller is automatically set to the " Smoke " setting.

The target smoke temperature ranges from 180 ° F / 82 ° C to 225 ° F / 17 ° C.

You can smoke food or raise the temperature to start cooking. Cooking temperatures range from 200 ° F to 500 ° F.

You can increase or decrease the T in 25 ° steps.

What types of cooking does the Pit Boss Grill offer?

In contrast to other grills, the Pit Boss Grill offers a cooking performance of 8-1. That means there is a lot more you can do than just grill your food. Pit Boss simplifies food preparation in the following ways:

1. Grill
2. Charles grill
3. Extinguish
4. Roast meat
5. Bbq
6. Cook
7. To grab

8. Smoke

What can be prepared on the Pit Boss pellet grill?

Anything you can cook or bake in the oven can be done with a smokehouse, according to Pete Boss.

You can cook meat, vegetables, seafood, fish, pork, vegetables, corn on the cob, potatoes, etc. You can bake cookies, sourdough bread, pancakes, and more!

Of course, you may need accessories like a cast iron pan, baking sheet, etc. If you don't know what to cook, check out the recipes on the Pit Boss website.

There are many cuts of Steak, and each of them has its characteristics.

The Sirloin (T-Bone)

The Sirloin can be recognized by its T-shaped bone and is most often called the T-Bone. It is a significant slice taken against the grain of the filet mignon. This piece is exceptionally tender, and its bone gives the meat a lot of flavors. T-Bone is popular because it combines portions of tenderloin and strip loin. It is so tasty that there is no need to marinate it. All you have to act is put spices it to taste. We find the strip loin in the same region, a tender cut located on the other side of the filet mignon.

The against-net

From the same region as sirloin, steak fillet Counter has denser fibers than the coast or the net. This piece presents a good balance between its marbling and its tenderness. Striploin has a slightly nutty flavor and is known to be juicy and tender. This cut is sometimes called the New York steak.

Filet mignon

Everyone knows about filet mignon! This is the very prized cut of beef. Filet mignon is both softer and leaner than other steaks. Coming from the loin, it is the most expensive piece because of the demand and its scarcity. It is said that a whole beef has only 3.5 kg of filet mignon. Filet mignon is not necessarily the tastiest of steaks, but it is undoubtedly the most tender.

BEEF CUTS

The entry stripped and sirloin

The Steak comes from the front of the bull, near the coast, and it is a part very tender, though a little more fat than other cuts. It is called the sirloin steak when the bone is removed from the cut. Many people love rib eye and entrecote because they are marbled steaks bursting with flavor. It is a juicy, tasty and tender piece that we season to taste to appreciate it fully.

The Top Sirloin Steak

The **sirloin** steak is classified as the classic Steak and exceptionally the most economical. It is also called the Boston steak. Its quality is good, and it is relatively tender and tasty. It does not contain any bone, is not marbled and has the advantage of being lean. It can be served as a steak, but it goes very well in the composition of various dishes: kebabs, Asian dishes, tacos, etc.

The flank steak

The flank steak comes from the sides of the beef (bottom sirloin) and offers a characteristic filamentous texture. The bib was mainly popularized in restaurants and has become very popular with consumers. It is pretty tough meat.

FISH CUTS

What are the different cuts of fish?

Your suppliers can offer you exclusive products or prepared them according to your needs. To facilitate your choices, you will find below information on the names used for the products on sale:

Whole: fish without any preparation.

Full: fish not empty.

Empty: fish whose viscera were abducted and whose abdominal cavity was cleansed.

Gutted with head (VAT): gutted fish with head.

Gutted decapitated (VDK): eviscerated fish with the head and gills removed.

Net: product from an operation of mechanical or manual threading. It is a muscle band taken from fish, characterized by its preparation:
- Fillet with skin or without skin
- Fillet with flaking skin
- Net with or without flank
- Boneless fillet

Steak: thick slice cut across the width containing the main ridge, "dorsal ridge."

Back: the dorsal part of the fish, which is the most fleshy and devoid of bones.

Pave: these slices cut in nets big fish. Tail drop or collar drop should not be considered a "cobblestone."

Papillon, Butterfly or Portefeuille or Double net: the two fillets of the fish are connected by the dorsal skin.

Trim: operations to rid the fish fillet of its waste (bones, fins, flanks, skin, etc.). Different trim levels range from A to E.
- Trim A: net or pavement edges without ridges and ventral edges.
- Trim B: fillet or pavé without a dorsal fin, slightly degreased.
- Trim C: net or pavé without a dorsal fin, wholly degreased.
- Trim D: fillet or pavé without a dorsal fin, degreased, without ridges.
- Trim E: fillet or pavé s without a dorsal fin, degreased, boneless and skinless.

LAMB CUTS

Whether it's a leg, stew or rack: lamb meat is very varied and can be prepared in many ways. The misconception that lamb meat tastes strong is wrong. If you cook it according to our advice, it will be delicious.

Swiss lamb meat experiences two seasonal peaks: the supply is highest in spring and early autumn. This is directly linked to sheep farming and its natural cycles. In Switzerland, most lambs are born between December and March. Racks and legs are thus already available shortly before Easter. When the lambs spend the summer months on pasture, they are slaughtered in September and October. Almost half of them are alpine lambs.

Here you will find the best way to cook the different pieces:

The neck

The lamb meat from the neck is intensely marbled. It contains a significant portion of fat. This part of the lamb is ideal for stewed dishes such as a hotpot or a stew. The neck is also a good choice for particularly aromatic minced meat.

Shoulder

The shoulder of lamb is an inexpensive piece. It contains less fat than the neck or chest. Rolled as a roast, like a sausage or cold meats, and as a stew or goulash, the shoulder can be prepared in a surprising variety of ways.

Chops

You can find chops individually or tied together in a rack. The fat layer brings a lot of flavors. If it's essential, you should only remove it after cooking - to prevent the meat from drying out.

Chest

The breast has long fibers finely interwoven with fat. The tip of lamb breast is often cut as a whole piece to be grilled, for example. Lamb's breast is readily cooked as a stew and hotpot.

The net

The most valuable piece of lamb is the tenderloin. This meat is lean, has short fibers and is very tender. It is best to sear it over high heat or place it on a hot grill. The tenderloin is perfectly pink - that is to point - when the meat thermometer indicates 60 ° C.

The lamb

We give the name of the leg to the back thighs of the lamb. This piece is available with or without bone and can be prepared whole or cut into slices. The bone maintains the meat during cooking and gives it extra flavor. Diced, the leg of lamb is ideal for meat fondues.

Shank

The meat of the lamb shank has a solid and aromatic taste. You can bake it in a single piece in the oven or simmer it. Thanks to its high proportion of connective tissue, the shank is also suitable for preparing stocks or sauces.

PORK CUTS

All over the world, it is one of the most appreciated animals from a culinary aspect. We get all kinds of cuts that we love. Bacon, ribs, ham, to name a few. Let's see where they come from.

Head

At first glance, it may seem repulsive to eat a whole pig's head, but it is nevertheless delicious, especially when roasted. The pig's head also includes tasty cuts in separate pieces, like the ears, tongue, cheeks and jowls. But we wouldn't judge you for not daring!

Shoulder

The pork butt is pulled from the upper part of the shoulder and back. The plowshare is the meat found around the spine in this section of the back. This cut of pork is ideal for successful and delicious pulled pork.

Loin

The pork loin is probably the part of the animal that is used the most for food. It is one of the most tender meats. It is used in countless recipes.

Maillard pork loin products

Pork fillet

Pork chops

Brochettes de porc

Pork loin roast

Rack of pork

Buttock

Pork buttocks are often used when talking about braised pork. It is also used for ham and cutlets, among others.

Maillard pork buttock products

Osso Buco

Picnic shoulder

The picnic shoulder got from the bottom part of the pork shoulder, very close to the breast. Since a pig's shoulder is part of a pig's leg and walks on all fours a lot, the picnic shoulder is very muscular. You can therefore cook it longer for a better result.

Maillard pork picnic shoulder products

Pork butt roast

Raised side of the flank

There is a difference between ribs on the flank and ribs on the back. Those on the side are longer and have a little meat between the bones. Those on the back, pulled from the loin, are shorter but have meat surrounding the bones as well. They are called "ribs" because they are "lifted" from the carcass at the very end. Flank ribs are also what are sometimes called *spareribs*.

Flank

The pork belly is the belly and breast of the animal. This cut of pork is undoubtedly the juiciest and most tender. It is from this part that bacon, bacon, pancetta, etc., are produced.

Maillard pork belly products

Bacon

Shank

Pork knuckles are generally used in cooking dishes such as pot roasts. Pulled from the legs, the shanks feature a very thick rind, making them very tasty meat.

CHICKEN CUTS

There are several ways to prepare Poulet. Whether you want to cook the wings, thighs, breasts or even the whole animal, everyone seems to agree on the rich taste and the omnipresent tenderness of the meat of this poultry.

It is essential to know where each part comes from. This also allows us to choose better the part we want when it comes time to shop for a good chicken recipe.

Neck

We obviously won't be talking about the head of the chicken, so let's move on to the animal's neck immediately. Most people throw this part away, but you might be missing out on something if you do because it's tasty, tender, and it costs next to nothing. We suggest a rillette recipe.

Chest

The chicken breast is, of course, one of the most stressed parts of the animal. Also called the supreme, the chicken breast is always tender. In addition, it is used in several sauces. As is, roasted, stewed, stuffed, on skewers.

Maillard chicken breast products

Chicken breasts

Chicken tournedos

Back

It is rarer that only the back of the chicken will be sold. In general, this part can be eaten by purchasing a whole chicken, such as a frog chicken.

Maillard chicken back products

Crapaudine chicken

Wing

The chicken wing has three parts. First, there is the pestle - or mini-pestle, smaller than the leg pestle. Then there's the fin, which is probably everyone's favorite piece. Less "meaty," but the taste of the crispy chicken skin is second to none. Finally, there is the tip of the wing. You will rarely find the latter in your packages of chicken wings, except because it contains much less meat than its sidekicks.

Chicken Wing Maillard Products

Chicken wings

Upper thigh

Chicken thighs sit between the animal's leg and its tail. Slightly fatter than the breast, this chicken cut is smooth, juicy and, thanks to the fat, extremely tasty. It is eaten very well grilled or roasted.

Maillard chicken thigh products

Chicken thighs

Leg

The chicken leg is another foodie favorite. It is also fatter than the breast; the portion of the chicken includes the leg and the thigh of the bird. So juicy, the fat gives it a most appreciable flavor. You'll be salivating at the thought of any recipe for chicken thighs or drumsticks.

THE DIFFERENT TYPES OF SALT

Big, delicate, plain or flavored, salt is now a staple in seasoning, and we use it almost every day.

FINE SALT

The most common of all salts is the one you always have on hand at home in your mill, a salt hand or a salt shaker on the table. It allows food to be salted in depth.

COARSE SALT

Its main characteristic lies in its large crystals, which are born from the very slow evaporation of water.

It is commonly used to saltwater at the start of cooking. It can also be added at the end of cooking to add crunch to the preparation.

Use it on a grilled piece of beef for good to make a salt crust, for example.

FLEUR DE SEL

Guérande salt, the best salt there is! The fleur de sel is formed on the surface of salt marshes; it is composed of tiny crystals of very pure white. Its particularity is that it retains a specific humidity.

The fleur de sel cannot be cooked; simply sprinkle it on your preparation before tasting. You will be able to enjoy all its crunchiness and its flavors.

FLAVORED SALTS

Vary the flavors by seasoning your dishes with flavored salts. You can buy them pre-made or prepare them yourself: salt with herbs, Espelette pepper, lemon … anything is possible!

Preferably use coarse salt as a base. For a good balance of flavors, count 1/3 of salt for 2/3 of dried aromatic herbs and approximately 70 g of salt for 30 g of spices.

HIMALAYAN PINK SALT

This earth salt is considered the purest salt in the world because it is neither iodized nor refined. Its pink color is due to its high iron content.

It can be used everywhere, like a classic salt. It is slightly less salty than a fleur de sel but more than traditional sea salt.

MARINADES

The main marinades

Meat marinade is a mixture of liquids and condiments in which all kinds of foods are left to stay for a short time, especially red and white meats and offal. There are two main categories of marinades: "long," raw or cooked, and "instant."

- **"Long" marinades** are intended to accommodate meats in a container for several hours or even several days before generally braised cooking. They are prepared with three types of ingredients:

liquids such as wine (red or white), vinegar, oils or alcohols;

of spices (garlic, pepper, salt, herbs, parsley stems);

vegetables (carrots, shallots, onions) cut into small pieces.

These marinades are most commonly made from raw ingredients, but they can also sometimes be cooked.

- **"Instant" marinades** are prepared more quickly. They sometimes only have two or three ingredients (oil and rosemary, for example). They are intended to be coated on meats just a few minutes before cooking, usually in a pan, grill, or barbecue.

The interest of the marinade for meat

Marinades are always used to flavor meats before cooking. But they have other virtues. We have long known their ability to tenderize the fibers of meats with a high level of collagen.

Marinades are long and commonly used to make even softer **pieces to slow cook** the **beef,** the **lamb** or the **horse**. But the practice of marinating has also developed with the development of the use of barbecue and plancha. It, therefore, has the advantage of protecting the fibers of the pieces of meat exposed to intense heat and of keeping the juice inside.

Finally, the marinade can be used to "cook" under the effect of acidic ingredients such as lemon or vinegar, meats are eaten raw, such as carpaccio and tartare.

Marinades and meat, instructions for use

The marinade can last from a few tens of minutes to several hours. The **red meat** (beef, lamb) supports extended marinades, while **white meats** (veal, pork) are fond of pickles. If the goal is to tenderize the meat, we will opt for a long bath, especially oversized pieces. If the goal is only to flavor the meat before going to the barbecue, a few tens of minutes are enough.

How long to let meats marinate?

For **roast beef**, pork, horse roast beef, leg of lamb weighing one kilogram or more, marinate for 10 to 24 hours (for example, the night before the day of cooking).

For detailed pieces of 40 to 50 grams of beef (Burgundy or cheek) or lamb (shoulder, leg), marinate for at least 5 hours (or even overnight).

For small pieces to grill or fry beef, lamb or veal, marinate for 1 to 2 hours.

For **beef**, lamb or offal **skewers**, marinate for 30 minutes to 1 hour.

Meat-marinade pairings: the recipes

In general, red meats like solid flavors, white meats (veal, pork), more discreet and lighter mixes. White meats are well suited to sweet and savory mixtures.

Marinade for the beef

For beef bourguignon or beef cheek: red wine, onions, carrots, cloves, pepper.

For the shank or the tab: soy sauce, ginger, red wine.

Marinade for the veal

For barbecue veal: onion, garlic, honey, soy sauce, vegetable oil, or masala.

Marinade for the pork

For slices of pork or ribs: Teriyaki (mirin, soy, sake, sugar, oil).

Marinade for the lamb

For **lamb** shoulder cubes: yogurt, lemon juice, olive oil, spices, coriander.

Marinade for tripe products

For beef heart (on a skewer): wine vinegar, red pepper, onion, garlic.

Marinade for horse meat

For **horse** roast beef: red wine, onion, carrot, bay leaf.

BRINE

What is brine?

Practical definition: Brine is the act of putting food, ranging from cheese to olives, including vegetables or ham, in salted water.

Of course, not just any saltwater; there are rules to follow.

Why do we brine before cooking?

Originally, brining was used for food preservation in the era of pre-refrigeration.

Without refrigeration, food would rot or ferment much faster. Fortunately, the discovery of using a solution composed of water and salt (or sodium chloride) has made it possible to lengthen the shelf life of many products, such as olives which are indeed the most famous recipe.

Nowadays, there are more reasons than conservation in a recipe: flavor and texture. The brining infuses the meat with savory, finger-licking flavors while tenderizing it with a soft, buttery texture.

How does it work?

This is how brining works: When you place meat in a bath of salty, aromatic liquid (in this case, water), the solution moves through the meat to equalize the salt levels.

This means that even before being heated, your meat has a higher liquid content. So when you cook it, it loses the same amount of moisture, but it's juicier.

As Harold McGee, culinary expert and food science expert, says: "This is your chance to see that our old nemesis, water retention, is playing a beneficial role! "

While you are bringing your meat, it doesn't just gain liquid, it also gains salt, and the higher concentration of salt will start to break down its protein.

Think of the protein in meat as tight, stubborn coils - the salt comes in, gives them a deep massage, and they begin to relax. The meat is then softer in the mouth and less hard to chew.

You can then pass the food to the smoker or make preserves in jars since the brine has already had its antibacterial effect.

What meat should be brined?

Some meats benefit more than others from bringing.

Drier, leaner meats top the list because they don't have much fat to contribute to moisture and flavor. Chicken breasts, pork chops, shrimp, and the famous Thanksgiving turkey are all good candidates for bringing.

As barbecue season approaches, squares of chops are begging to be soaked in the brine, which will help them retain their moisture during a long smoker. Before purchasing a piece of meat for bringing, check the label to make sure it hasn't already been injected with a saline solution.

How long does it take time to brine meat?

The meat should be left in the brine for about an hour per half a kilogram as a rule of thumb. Never exceed the prescribed brining time to prevent the protein from breaking down too much and the meat turning into an unappetizing porridge.

I have already tried for you; I guarantee you that it is not good. 24his a good indication for large parts.

How to brine meat

The basic formula for any wet brine is 225g of salt to 3.78L of water.

If you're feeling fancy, add crushed garlic cloves, peppercorns, citrus (also crushed), or even a sweetener like honey or brown sugar.

Pro tip: if your meat has skin (hi, turkey), drain it, then pat it dry a few hours before cooking and leave it in the fridge, uncovered. It will be juicy and tender, with incredibly crispy skin.

What is dry brine?

Dry brining is a technically incorrect definition.

The definition "brining" implies a liquid, and dry brining could instead be thought of as a rub, or "cure," for your meat. However, the result is quite similar. You redistribute the moisture and penetrate the seasoning deep into the meat by coating your meat in a salted mixture.

How to dry brine meat

The general dry brining technique uses 1/2 teaspoon of kosher salt per pound of meat, along with any other (dried) herbs and spices you want. Reduce everything to a sandy texture with a mortar and pestle, then rub your meat. It is pretty simply salting, as has been done in the French gastronomic heritage for a long time.

This salting is the basis of ham and other recipes involving a large piece of pork or other.

RUB

Rubs are a collection of spices, herbs, and seasonings used to coat the outside of the meat. The basis of a rub is salt, with which additional ingredients are combined, among which the most used is sugar. There are no accurate rules for deciding which spices or herbs to add; it depends on your taste. The best time to apply the rub is 15 minutes before cooking so that the meat has time to absorb the flavors. However, the time could be even longer in the case of particularly tough or flavorful types of meat. To apply the rub, I recommend first covering the core with a drizzle of olive oil, then with one hand, pour the rub on the meat and rub the beef vigorously with the other hand. The rub should be applied evenly over the entire surface of the meat.

MEAT SMOKING GUIDE

MEAT TYPE	SMOKING TEMPERATURE	TIME	INTERNAL TEMPERATURE
Brisket (6 to 12 lbs)	250° F	1 H/lb	195°F
Chuck roast	250°F	1.5 H/lb	195°F
Prime rib medium	225°F	15 Mins/lb	135°F
Ribs (full rack)	225°F	4 to 5 H	175°F
Roast Medium	225°F	3 to 4 H	145°F
Rump Roast	250°F	30 Mins/lb	145°F
Sirloin Tips Roast medium	250°F	8 H	140°F
Tenderloin medium rare	225°F	2 to 3 H	140°F
Veal chops	200°F	1.5 H/lb	160°F

POULTRY

MEAT TYPE	SMOKING TEMPERATURE	TIME	INTERNAL TEMPERATURE
Chicken (whole) 3 to 5 lbs	250°F	1 H/lb	165°F
Chicken Breasts (Bone-in)	225°F	1H	165°F
Chicken Breasts (Boneless)	225°F	45 Mins./lb	165°F
Chicken Thigh	225°F	2 H	165°F
Turkey (Whole) 8 to 12 lbs	225°F	30 to 35 Mins/lb	165°F
Turkey Breast/legs	250°F	3.5 to 4 H	165°F

MEAT TYPE	SMOKING TEMPERATURE	TIME	INTERNAL TEMPERATURE
Butt (Pulled) 6 to 12 lb	250°F	1,5 H/lb	195°F
Ham (Bone in)	250°F	1,5 H/lb	160°F
Hog (Whole) to 85 lb	250°F	16 to 18 H	205°F
Ribs (Baby Back)	225°F	4 to 5 H	165°F
Ribs (Spare ribs)	225°F	5 to 7 H	190°F
Sausage 1,5 to 2,5 inch	225°F	1 to 3 H	160°F
Shoulder (Pulled) 6 to 10lbs	250°F	8 to 12 H	190°F
Tenderloin 1.5 to 2 lbs	225°F	2.5 to 3 H	160°F

MEAT TYPE	SMOKING TEMPERATURE	TIME	INTERNAL TEMPERATURE
Fishes (Filless) 2 lbs	225°F	35 to 45 Mins	145°F
Salmon	200°F	2.5 to 3 H	145°F
Shrimp	225°F	1 to 2 H	145°F

HOW TO PREPARE YOUR PIT ON

Several pellets required If you use the quick grilling method, keep as a reference that you will need four pounds of pellets for every hour of grilling. If on the other side, you intend to smoke with low and slow smoke, you will need approximately two pounds of pellets every hour. - Turn on the PIT Once you have loaded the pellets, open the lid and set it to "smoke." Your PIT will feed the pellets for about four minutes and then stop. This maneuver allows the igniter to spark and subsequently feed more fuel. During these four minutes, you should see thick clouds of smoke. This is the sign that the pellets are burning. After four minutes, the smoke will reduce. After a few times, you will listen to the sound of the fire, and from this moment, you can raise the temperature. It will take another 5 - 8 minutes before the set temperature is reached. Now, you are ready!

How to SMOKE LIKE A PIT MASTER

Are you a barbecue lover? Cooking becomes festive when it comes to barbecue. When it comes to grilling, you must also use the best grilling machine.

Why should you use a pellet grill?

Pellet Smoker Grill is an easy and safe option for all grill items. You can set the appropriate temperature and leave the food you want to grill inside. The machine also contains wood, allowing it to give it a smoky flavor on the grill.

This means that it heats the environment around your food to improve taste and flavor. This is very important for large pieces of Steak. Indirect heat allows it to cook well, and the meat becomes juicier after long hours of heating.

Fire up your wood pellet grill

Follow a few simple rules to start the Pit Boss Pellet Grill. Follow the guide and enjoy the most delicious meals from your smoked grill like a perfectionist.

1. Fill the hopper with fuel.

It looks a lot like your vehicle. Add fuel before starting a new trip. Instead of gas, add wood pellets for fuel before you begin cooking. You must use at least two pounds of wood pellets during one hour of cooking.

Once the hopper is full of fuel, it's time to smoke your grills. Grills typically consume pellets in 3-4 minutes and then turn off. This opens up a chance to get it started before it runs out of fuel.

If you set high temperatures like 300 degrees Fahrenheit or higher, it will continue to feed on pellets until it reaches that temperature. If no fuels are available, it would be difficult to light it. Therefore, there is a possibility that the granules will accumulate in the pot. Make sure to clean it up. Otherwise, it may spill all over the place.

2. Prepare your food

It is best to prepare the grills in advance. To intensify the flavor and flavor, marinate the meat a few hours before. The Pit Boss grill will light up in no time. It takes about three minutes for things to heat up.

3. Beware of the smoke

How do you know your grill is on the right track? You will see thick clouds of smoke. This is a clear indication that it has caught fire and that the wood pellets are burning. This smoke can alarm your neighbors. To avoid the drama, let them know it's just a grill.

4. Run it

After three to four minutes, the smoke will begin to dissipate. Now is the time to start grilling. You will likely listen to the roar of the fire once it reaches the pot. This happens due to the fan blowing into the grill. There is no need to be afraid! Raise it to the desired temperature and begin your mission. It should reach the set temperature within five to six minutes.

Choose the meat

Cuts of meat have a significant impact on their flavor and tenderness. Before eating a steak, it is necessary to know the different types of cuts of meat.

1. Rib steaks

It can be boned or with bones. This meat comes from the rib section of the cow. However, it contains a lot of fat and serves as individual fillets.

2. Skirt steak

Flank steak or London grill is the meat under the loin and sirloin region of the cow. It is mainly fibrous throughout its length. Skirt steak is also known as skirt steak.

3. Skirt steak

Skirt steak originates from the cow's diaphragm muscles. Its fiber crosses the entire width of the Steak. This Steak is meatier than flank.

4. Steak

It is the most popular type of all the steak variations. It comes from the region of the cow's tenderloin or short sirloin. Includes T-shaped lumbar vertebrae with muscle fibers.

5. Filet mignon

Filet mignon, or filet mignon, is a boneless steak. It is also the most costly of all the options. It comes from the region of the short loin and the sirloin of the cow. You can also make the Steak softer and juicier with tenderloin steaks. In another record, it is the same.

GRILL GUIDE:	POULTRY	SEAFOOD	LAMB	PORK	BEEF	VEGGIES
GOURMET BLEND	✓	✓	✓	✓	✓	✓
HICKORY	✓		✓	✓	✓	✓
MESQUITE	✓	✓		✓	✓	
APPLE	✓	✓		✓		✓
CHERRY	✓	✓	✓	✓	✓	
OAK		✓	✓	✓	✓	✓
PECAN	✓		✓	✓	✓	
MAPLE	✓			✓		✓
ALDER	✓	✓		✓		

1700 DAYS

Should you be wondering 1700 Days what exactly means -- here it is explained! Thoughtfully crafted for their benefits, the recipes in this cookbook when mixed and spread out over the day's meals are enough to guarantee you all those days of healthy, clean eating! All you have to do at this point is find your favorites and begin your journey to a new-tritious lifestyle.

BREAKFAST

SMOKED PEACHES

Prep T: 5 mins /**Cook T**: 30 mins /**Serves**: 4

Ingredients:

- 4 halved peaches
- 2 cups vanilla ice cream

Directions:

1.Preheat smoker to 200° with wood chips in the container. Put peaches in a foil pan, with the cut-side facing up.

2.Put in the smoker for 20 minutes, and then flip the peaches. Smoke for another 10 minutes. Serve with ice cream!

SMOKED CHEESECAKE

Prep T: 30 mins /**Cook T:** 2 h /**Serves:** 8-10
Ingredients:

- 12-ounces graham crackers
- 3 tablespoons brown sugar
- 6 tablespoons melted butter
- 32-ounces room-temp cream cheese
- 1 packed cup light brown sugar
- 2 teaspoons pure vanilla extract
- 1 teaspoon orange zest
- 5 eggs
- 1 tablespoon fresh orange juice
- 2 tablespoons melted butter

Directions:
1.Preheat oven to 400°. Grease a springform pan and line inside with foil. Begin by making the crust. 2.Put graham crackers in a food processor and pulse into a fine powder with brown sugar.
3.Pulse in melted butter to get a crumbly dough that you can press into the pan, and it sticks. Bake in the oven within 5-8 minutes, until golden. Move to a rack and cool. Warm your smoker to 300°.
4.For the filling, mix cream cheese, 1 cup of sugar, vanilla, and orange zest in a mixer until smooth. Add eggs - one at a time - and orange juice until smooth.
5.Pour batter into the pan. Put the cheesecake in the smoker, uncovered, and smoke within 1 ½- 2 hours.
6.Cheesecake is done when the filling jiggles but is firm, like jello. Move cheesecake to the counter and cool to room temperature. Cover with saran wrap, then chill in the fridge for at least 4 hours, No serve warm!

BAKED CANDIED BACON CINNAMON ROLLS

Prep T: 10 mins /**Cook T:** 35 mins /**Serves:** 6
Ingredients:

- 12 Bacon slices
- .33 or 1/3 cup Brown sugar
- Pre-made cinnamon rolls
- 2 oz. or 56 g Unchilled cream cheese
- Suggested Pellets: Apple
- Also Needed: 8x8-inch or 20x20-cm baking dish or cake pan

Directions:
1.Set the Pit Boss to 350°F and wait to acquire its temperature setting. Dredge eight of the bacon slices through the sugar. Place *all* of the bacon on a metal rack placed on a big baking tray. Smoke the bacon until the fat renders, but the bacon is still pliable (15-20 min.). Then, adjust the Boss temperature to 325°F. Unroll the cinnamon rolls and add a bacon slice - close it. Continue with the rest of the rolls.
2.Spritz the baking tray with cooking spray and add the rolls to the pan. Cook the cinnamon rolls at 325° Fahrenheit until nicely browned (10-15 min.). Rotate the tray after about 6-7 minutes. Use the cream cheese frosting (from the roll pkg.) and mix in the cream cheese.
3.Crumble the rest of the bacon and mix it in with the cream cheese frosting. Slather the prepared frosting over warm rolls and serve.

BAKED BREAKFAST SAUSAGE CASSEROLE

Prep T: 30 mins /**Cook T**: 2 h /**Serves**: 8
Ingredients:
- 1 tbsp. Olive oil or vegetable oil
- 2 medium Red or green bell peppers
- 1 medium Yellow onion
- 3 tsp. + more as needed Kosher salt - divided
- 1 lb. Thick-cut bacon
- 1 lb. or 450 g Ground breakfast sausage
- 2 lb. or 910 g Shredded hash browns or tater tots - defrosted
- 3 cups Shredded medium cheddar cheese - divided
- 10 large Eggs
- .5 cup Milk
- 1 tsp. + as needed Black pepper
- Pellets Suggested: Pecan

Also Needed: Cast-iron skillet & 9x13-inch/9x33-cm baking dish
Directions:
1.Set the Pit Boss temperature to preheat at 350°F, adding the skillet to heat, pour oil (1 tbsp.) in the pan when heated. Dice and add the onion and peppers with salt (1 tsp.). Sauté them for about 20 minutes, stirring at 5–7-minute intervals till they're softened.
2.Meanwhile, add the bacon to the Boss and grill till it's crispy (25-30 min.). Drain and chop the bacon into bite-sized chunks. Once the veggies are ready, add the sausage, grilling till done (8-10 min.).
3.Load a big mixing container with the tater tots/hash browns, sausage, bacon, peppers, and onions with a shake of black pepper and salt. Sprinkle the cheese (1.5 cups) over the top and thoroughly mix, adding it to the baking dish.
4.Use a separate mixing container to whisk the eggs with the milk pepper (1 tsp.) and salt (2 tsp.). Add the eggs over the fixings in the baking dish. Wait for about five minutes and dust with the rest of the cheese. Cover the casserole dish with a layer of foil. Bake it for 45 minutes in the Pit Boss. Discard the piece of foil and continue baking till the cheese is bubbling. Serve with a smile!

SMOKED CHEESE AND BACON EGG BITES

Prep T: 15 mins /**Cook T**: 1 h /**Serves**: 6
Ingredients:
- 1/4 cup of milk
- 12 slices of bacon
- 1/4 cup of shredded Cheese
- Nine eggs

Directions:
1.Season the bacon with barbecue seasoning & smoke it for around 30 to 45 minutes to 225°F, using a nonstick spray, coat each cup of a 12 tin muffin tray. Using the cut bacon, line a muffin pan.
2.In a large-sized mixing dish, combine the remaining ingredients, fill each muffin pan about two-thirds full with the egg mixture. Cook the egg bits in the smoker for 15 minutes at 400°F.

BREAKFAST SMOKED CASSEROLE

Prep T: 35 mins /**Cook T**: 35 mins /**Serves**: 4

Ingredients:
- 1 cup of diced onions
- 2 cups of Shredded Cheese
- 1 tablespoon of olive oil
- 2 lbs. of ground pork sausages
- One package of Crescent Dough Sheet
- 1 cup of diced assorted color bell peppers
- One tablespoon of hot sauce
- 1 cup of sliced Mushrooms
- Salt and pcppcr to taste
- Ten eggs large
- 1 cup of sour cream
- 1 tablespoon of butter

Directions:

1.On medium heat, brown 2 pounds of pork sausage & drain on a paper towel-lined plate. In a large-sized skillet, melt one tablespoon of butter and one tablespoon of olive oil & sauté veggies until soft, about 3 to 4 minutes. Mix sausage and 1 cup of onion, 1 cup of assorted color bell peppers, & 1 cup of mushroom and set them aside.

2.Break 10 Large Egg and beat in a large-sized mixing dish. Mix in 2 cups of shredded cheese, one tablespoon hot sauce, 1 cup sour cream, and a sprinkle of salt and black pepper (to taste). To mix the ingredients, whisk them together, arrange Crescent Dough Sheet (1 box) in the bottom of a 9X11 inch baking sheet sprayed with cooking spray. Evenly distribute the sausage and veggies throughout the dough, then top with the egg mixture.

3.Refrigerate the dish for approximately 1 hour before serving. Preheat the pellet grill or other smoker to 350°F for cooking. Arrange casserole and cook for around 1 hour on a barbeque pit, moving the pan every 30 minutes to ensure equal grilling, the dish is done when the top is golden and the sides come away from the pan slightly. Remove the fruit from the pit and cut it into serving sizes. Serve with your favorite toppings.

SMOKED TASTY BREAKFAST FATTY

Prep T: 15 mins /**Cook T**: 10 mins /**Serves**: 6
Ingredients:
- 2 cups of prepared hash browns
- 1 pound of bacon
- 1 pound of breakfast sausage
- 1 tablespoon of rub
- 1 cup of shredded Colby jack cheese

Directions:
1.Preheat the pellet grill to 250°F according to the manufacturer's instructions. If you're using a different style of grill, ensure it's set to indirect heat.
2.Make a bacon weave on top of a sheet of plastic wrap using the entire pound of bacon and leave aside. If you're not sure how to build a bacon weave, follow these steps.
3.Place the plastic wrap on the counter and pat out the morning sausage into a 6x6 square. Over the top, layer the hash browns & Cheese and gently press down.
Roll the sausage into a log, like a cinnamon roll.
4.Carefully place the sausage roll on top of the bacon weave using the plastic wrap, then roll out the plastic wrap, so it is on front of the bacon.
5.Wrap the bacon weave around the fatty and tie it together with the butcher's twine, or gently put it on a sheet of non stick foil (taking away the plastic wrap) and grill it.
6.Cook, occasionally rotating until the bacon is crispy and the internal temperature reaches 165°, remove from the grill, set aside for 10 minutes, then slice & serve.

TASTY BREAKFAST GRILLED PIZZA

Prep T: 35 mins /**Cook T**: 20 mins /**Serves**: 6

Ingredients:

- 8 oz. of bulk breakfast sausage
- six eggs large
- 1/4 cup of olive oil
- 3/4 teaspoon of kosher salt
- 1 lb. of refrigerated pizza dough
- one small chopped onion
- 2 cups of shredded mozzarella cheese
- Chopped fresh chives for garnishing
- two chopped bell peppers (1 red and one green)
- Black pepper, to taste
- 2 cups of frozen and shredded hash browns, thawed & squeezed dry

Directions:

1.Preheat the grill to medium-high temperature. 2 tablespoons olive oil, brushed over an upside-down baking sheet, Place the pizza dough on the greased side of the pan in an 11-by-14-inch rectangle.

2.On the grill, heat one tablespoon of olive oil in a large-sized cast-iron pan. Cook, splitting up the sausage into pieces and turning regularly until the flesh is no longer pink, for four to five minutes. 3.Remove to a platter with a slotted spoon. Add the bell peppers & onion to the skillet & cook, occasionally turning, for 3 to 4 minutes, or until the veggies soften.

4.Add the hash browns, half teaspoon of salt, and a few grinds of pepper, along with the leftover one tablespoon olive oil. Cook, occasionally tossing, for 2 to 3 minutes, or till the hash browns soften & begin to turn light golden brown. Place the sausage on top of the hash brown-vegetable combination on the dish. Take the skillet from the grill and set it aside.

5.Slide the dough off from the pan & onto the grill with care. Cook, uncovered, for 3 to 4 minutes, or until bubbles appear on top & the bottom is marked. 6.Turn the dough, marked-side up, onto the upside-down sheet pan with a big spatula.

7.Leave a 1/2-inch border around the dough while spreading the mozzarella. Distribute the hash brown−veggie mixture & sausage equally over the top. Make six tiny wells in the toppings with the back of a big spoon and delicately break an egg through each well. Slide the pizza back onto the grill after removing it from the pan.

8.Cover and cook for 12 minutes, or till the Cheese is melted & egg whites are set, but the yolks still are runny.

9.Place the pizza on a cutting board to cool. Add the rest of 1/4 teaspoon of salt & a few pinches of pepper to the eggs. Serve with chives as a garnish.

APPETIZERS

GRILLED CHICKEN WINGS

Prep T: 25 mins /**Cook T**: 40 mins /**Serves**: 6
Ingredients:
* 2-3 pounds full chicken wings
* 1 teaspoon lemon pepper seasoning
* favorite wing sauce (optional)

Directions:
1.Place chicken wings in pot and cover with water. Bring to boil and when water boils set timer for 10 minutes. Remove from heat, and skim off fat with large spoon before removing wings.
2.Place boiled wings on a pan to cool, after wings have cooled enough to handle, use a towel or two and wring out the excess water from the wings. 3.Squeeze the wing gently in the towel, just enough to dry it out a bit after boiling.
3.Toss lightly in lemon pepper seasoning, set the pellet grill at 425° using 100% Hickory Cookinpellets. Place chicken on grill and smoke for 35-40 minutes. Turn once at the 20 minute mark.
4.Check temperature and ensure that it is cooked through to 165°. Remove from grill when chicken is golden brown. Rest for 5 minutes - they will be very hot!

BACON-WRAPPED STUFFED PICKLES

Prep T: 60 mins /**Cook T:** 10 mins /**Serves:** 6
Ingredients:
- 13 strips bacon
- 3 bratwursts, raw
- 1/2 cup colby jack cheese, shredded
- 4 oz cream cheese
- 13 large dill pickles, spears
- Pit boss hickory bacon rub
- 2 scallion, sliced thin
- 1/4 cup sour cream

Directions:
1.Preheat grill to medium-low flame, in a mixing bowl, combine cream cheese, sour cream, and scallions, use a hand mixer to blend well, then fold in grated cheddar-jack. Set aside.
2.Cook bratwurst on the griddle. Use a metal spatula to chop up sausage into smaller bits and cook until browned. Remove from the grill and set aside on a sheet tray to cool. Place pickles on a sheet tray. Cut in half, then remove seeds with a small measuring spoon. Stuff one-half of each pickle with cream cheese mixture and to with crumbled bratwurst.
3.Top with the other pickle half, then wrap in bacon, season bacon-wrapped pickles with Hickory Bacon 5.Rub, place in cast iron skillet, then transfer to grill. Grill pickles for 45 to 55 minutes until bacon starts to crisp on top. Remove from grill. Serve warm.

APPLEWOOD BACON JALAPENO POPPERS

Prep T: 20 mins /**Cook T:** 30 mins /**Serves:** 6
Ingredients:
- 2 teaspoon pit boss applewood bacon seasoning
- 1 pack cheddar cheese, shredded
- 1 pack cream cheese, softened
- Cut in half lengthwise, destemmed, deveined and deseeded jalapeno peppers
- 8 strips smoked applewood bacon, cut in half

Directions:
1.In a large bowl, combine cream cheese, Applewood Bacon seasoning, and cheddar cheese. Mix until thoroughly combined.
2.Using a spoon, fill the peppers with the cream cheese mixture. Wrap each pepper with a half slice of bacon and secure with a toothpick. Repeat until all jalapeno poppers are finished.
3.Preheat your Pit Boss Grill to 400°F. Place your jalapeno poppers on the grill basket and grill for 15-20 minutes, or until the bacon is cooked and crispy. Serve and enjoy!

SMOKED ROSEMARY AND BLOOD ORANGE SPRITZ

Prep T: 10 mins /**Cook T:** 0 mins /**Serves:** 2
Ingredients:
- 4 blood oranges large, 1 sliced in rounds & 1 halved

For the simple rosemary syrup:
- 4 sprigs of rosemary
- 1 cup of water
- 1 cup of granulated sugar

For the cocktail:
- 3 ounces of Aperol
- 2 sprigs of rosemary for garnishing
- 2 ounces of blood orange juice
- 2 slices of grilled blood orange for garnishing
- 2 ounces of simple rosemary syrup

Directions:
1.When ready to cook, preheat the grill to 185°F with the lid closed for around 15 minutes. If Super Smoke is available, use it for the best flavor. Dissolve the sugar and water in a saucepan, then incorporate the rosemary and grill. On the barbecue grates, put the blood orange slices & halves. Smoke for 1 hour, or until they've begun to burn, and the simple syrup has taken on a lovely Smokey hue. Remove the pan from the grill and set it aside to cool fully.

2.Set aside the cooled orange pieces for decoration. Orange halves should be juiced, then strained, and the sediments discarded. To make the cocktail, load a cocktail shaker halfway with ice. Combine the simple rosemary syrup, blood orange juice, & Aperol. Shake & pour into your favorite wine glass, then top with prosecco. Serve with a grilled orange slice as well as a rosemary sprig for garnish. Enjoy!

GRILLED COCKTAIL WITH MELON

Prep T: 10 mins /**Cook T:** 0 mins /**Serves:** 2
Ingredients:
- 1 cup of turbinado sugar
- 2 ounces of cantaloupe juice
- 1/2 ounce of simple smoked syrup
- 3 ounces of reposado tequila
- 2 whole cantaloupe
- 1/2 ounce of lime juice
- Cherry wood smoked salt

Directions:
1.When ready to cook, preheat the grill to 500°F with the lid closed for around 15 minutes. Cantaloupe should be cut in half, and the seeds should be scooped out. One of the cantaloupe halves should be cut into wedges. Remove from the equation. Remove the rind from the other half & slice into 1-inch cubes. Puree the cantaloupe in a blender and filter through a mesh sieve. Set aside the liquid.

2.Place cantaloupe slices on a hot grill after coating them with turbinado sugar. 3 minutes per side on the grill, or till grill marks appear. Remove the wedges from the grill, quarter them into triangles, and set them aside.

3.Combine Smoked Simple Syrup, lime juice, smoked salt, 1 ounce of cantaloupe juice, and tequila in a cocktail shaker. 10 seconds in the shaker, then pour into a double rocks glass. Fill glass with crushed ice until it is completely full, serve with a piece of grilled cantaloupe as a garnish. Enjoy!

PIG IN A HAMMOCK COCKTAIL

Prep T: 10 mins /**Cook T:** 0 mins /**Serves**: 4

Ingredients:

- 12 ounces of pure maple syrup
- 8 ounces of fresh lemon juice
- 3 strips of bacon
- 1 pinch of salt
- 8 dash of Angostura bitters
- 3 whole ripe bananas
- 8 ounces of water
- 6 ounces of bourbon

Directions:

1.When you're ready to cook, preheat the grill to 350°F with the lid closed for around 15 minutes. Place bacon on a sheet pan in the center of the grill & cook for 20 minutes, or until desired crispness is achieved. Remove out of the grill and set aside to cool, increase the grill temperature to 500°F and cook for 15 minutes with the cover closed. 2.Peel bananas and lay them straight on the grill grate (in the grill's hottest areas) for 5 minutes per side, or until grill marks form. Remove them out of the grill and set them aside, in a small-sized saucepan on medium flame, bring 8 of ounces' water, maple syrup, and a sprinkle of salt to a simmer. Add two of the scorched bananas to the saucepan in half-moons.

3.Cook for 15 minutes before straining into a heat-resistant container. Make sure to scrape off as much of the syrup as possible off the bananas. Remove the bananas and place the syrup in the refrigerator to cool.

4.In a cocktail shaker, combine 1-1/2 of ounces' bourbon, 1 ounce of burnt maple/banana syrup, 1 ounce of lemon juice, and 2 dashes of Angostura Bitters. Shake for around 10 seconds after adding ice. 6Repeat with the remaining 3 drinks, straining into a coupe glass, serve with hal.f a slice of crispy bacon as a garnish. (You may eat the third slice of bacon as a snack!) The third banana should be sliced into slices and placed on top of every drink. Enjoy!

SMOKED TEXAS-STYLE RANCH WATER

Prep T: 10 mins /**Cook T:** 0 mins /**Serves**: 4

Ingredients:

- 24 ounces of Topo Chico
- 3 limes whole
- 12 ounces of Blanco tequila
- 8 slices of jalapeno
- 1 tablespoon of blackened Saskatchewan rub

Directions:

1.Set the grill to 225°F & preheat for 15 minutes with the lid closed when you're ready to cook, slice two limes in half and coat with Blackened Saskatchewan Rub. Position the 4 lime halves on the grill grate's edge and let them smoke for an hour.

2.Remove them from the grill and set them aside to cool. Pour a tiny amount of the rub onto a dish. Slice the third lime into 1/4 wedges, rub the rims of four cocktail glasses with the lime, then turn the glasses upside down & into the rub to salt the rims.

3.Pour 6 ounces Topo Chico, 3 ounces of tequila, squeeze of 1 smoked lime (throw away after squeezing), and one fresh lime wedge into each of your rimmed glasses over many ice cubes. Put one or two slices of jalapeno into each glass if using (muddle if desired). Mix to combine. Serve and enjoy!

BUBZ AND SMOKE COCKTAIL

Prep T: 10 mins /**Cook T**: 0 mins /**Serves**: 2
Ingredients:
- 2 teaspoons of pomegranate seeds
- 2 lemon twist for garnishing
- 6 ounces of sparkling white wine

For the smoked pomegranate juice:
- 2 cups of pomegranate seeds
- 16 ounces of POM juice

Directions:
1.Set the grill to 180°F & preheat for 15 minutes with the lid covered when you're ready to cook. If Super Smoke is available, use it for the best flavor.
2.To make the Smoked Pomegranate Juice, in a shallow sheet pan, combine POM juice & a cup of pomegranate seeds. Smoke for 45 minutes. Remove from the grill, squeeze off the seeds, and set aside to cool.
3.In the bottom of the champagne flute, pour 1-1/2 ounces of smoked pomegranate juice. To serve, garnish with sparkling white wine, just a few fresh pomegranate seeds, & a lemon twist. Enjoy!

SMOKE AND BEER COCKTAIL

Prep T: 10 mins /**Cook T**: 0 mins /**Serves**: 2
Ingredients:
- 1 teaspoon of Maggie seasoning sauce
- 2 teaspoons of HP original sauce
- 3 ounces of lime juice
- 1/8 ounce of Valentina Hot sauce
- 24 ounces of Mexican lager

Directions:
1.Set the grill on Smoke with the lid open till the fire is formed when you're ready to cook (4 to 5 minutes), in a shallow oven-safe dish, combine HP Original Sauce, 12 parts of spicy sauce, and Maggi Seasoning. Smoke for around 30 minutes by placing the dish straight on the grill grate.
2.Remove out from the grill and set aside to cool. In a chilled sal de gusano & salt-rimmed pint glass full of ice, combine all of the ingredients.

GRILLED FILET MIGNON

Prep T: 10 mins /**Cook T**: 20 mins /**Serves**: 1
Ingredients:
- Salt
- Pepper
- 3 Filet mignons

Directions:
1.Preheat your grill to 450°, season the steak with a good amount of salt and pepper to enhance its flavor. Place on the grill and flip after 5 minutes.
2.Grill both sides for 5 minutes each, take it out when it looks cooked and serve with your favorite side dish.

PORK RECIPES

GRILLED PEPPERCORN PORK CHOPS

Prep T: 10 mins /**Cook T**: 30 mins /**Serves**: 4

Ingredients:

- 1/4 cup of cumin
- 1 1/2 teaspoons of salt
- 1 teaspoon of olive oil
- 3 tablespoons of ground black peppercorns
- 4 bone-in pork chops
- 1 tablespoon of coriander seeds
- 2 tablespoons of sugar
- 1 to 2 teaspoons of dry rub

Directions:

1.Begin your grill on smoke and keep the lid open till a fire in the burn pot has formed (3-7 minutes), preheat the oven to 450°F, in a cast iron pan, add the cumin seeds, entire black peppercorns, & coriander seeds. Stir for around 8 minutes on medium flame until roasted. Allow for some cooling time. In a blender, finely crush the toasted spices & move to a small-sized bowl, then stir in the sugar and salt.

2.On all sides, rub the seasonings into the pork chops. Inside the grill, place a cast-iron skillet. When the skillet is heated, drizzle in the olive oil & coat the base. Season the pork chops with salt and pepper before placing them on the pan. Make sure each pork chop is separated from the others by a sufficient amount of space. Cook chops for 30 minutes. Switch off the grill after the pork chops are thoroughly cooked, remove the pan, dish, and enjoy!

RASPBERRY CHIPOTLE FLAVORED PORK KEBABS

Prep T: 60 mins /**Cook T**: 45 mins /**Serves**: 8

Ingredients:
- 3 sliced green bell pepper
- 1 chunked red onion
- 1 tablespoon of olive oil
- 1 lb. of boneless pork loin
- 1/8 cup of vinegar apple cider
- 8 skewers (12-inch)
- 2 tablespoons of Raspberry chipotle spice rub
- 1 tablespoon of honey

Directions:

1.Mix together apple cider vinegar, olive oil, Raspberry Chipotle spice, and honey in a medium mixing dish. Toss the cubed pork loin into the marinade & set it aside. Seal with plastic wrap & set aside for 30 to 1 hour to marinate.

2.Remove the meat from the marinade & insert pork cubed loin onto the skewers, alternately with bell pepper and red onion slices. Preheat the ceramic charcoal grill to 400°F.

3.Grill the kebabs direct on the grill, frequently rotating, until the pork is nicely browned on both sides and the veggies are soft (about 15 minutes). Serve right away. Note: Soak wooden skewers in water for around 30-45 minutes before using.

ROSEMARY GRILLED PORK CHOPS

Prep T: 180 mins /**Cook T**: 5 mins /**Serves**: 4

Ingredients:
- 4 pork chops
- 1 cup of soy sauce
- 6 tablespoons of brown sugar
- 1/2 cup of warm water
- 2 tablespoons of dried rosemary springs

Directions:

1.Combine the soy sauce, brown sugar, water, & rosemary in a mixing bowl, then pour half of the marinade into a plastic resealable bag. Remove any extra air and close the bag after adding the chops and coating them with the marinade. Set aside the leftover marinade and marinate the pork chops for approximately 3 hours.

2.Turn your grill on "smoke," with the lid wide open until a fire in the burn pot is formed (3-7 minutes)— Preheat at 350°F. Grease the grate lightly. Remove the pork chops out of the marinade and brush off any excess.

3.Grill the pork chops till they are not pink in the middle, approximately 4-5 minutes per side, or until done, brushing periodically with the leftover marinade. Serve the pork chops straight from the grill.

RASPBERRY FLAVORED SPIRAL HAM

Prep T: 10 mins /**Cook T:** 2 h /**Serves:** 12

Ingredients:

- Raspberry chipotle spice rub
- 1/4 cup of sugar
- 1/2 jar of raspberry jam
- 1/3 cup of warm water
- 1 precooked ham, spiral
- 1-quart fresh raspberry

Directions:

1.Preheat the grill to 225°F, rub the ham with raspberry chipotle spice, making sure to season each slice thoroughly. Place on the grill for roughly 2 hours to smoke.

2.Add the glaze ingredients in a saucepan on medium flame till raspberries are no longer whole & glaze is flowing, just before pulling the ham. If you'd like a smoother glaze, strain the glaze with cheesecloth to eliminate the raspberry seeds. Just before serving, drizzle the glaze over the ham. Slice and serve immediately. Enjoy!

CUBANO PORK SANDWICHES

Prep T: 10 mins /**Cook T:** 10 mins /**Serves:** 4

Ingredients:

- 1/4 cup of Dijon mustard
- Pulled pork rub
- 1 lb. of ham
- 3 cups of chicken stock
- 8 oz. of sliced Swiss cheese
- 1 sliced white onion
- 4 slice dill pickle
- 3 1/2 lbs pork shoulder
- 4 Ciabatta bread, halved
- 1 tablespoon of vegetable oil
- 1/4 cup of mayonnaise
- 1 tablespoon of butter

Directions:

1.Preheat your pellet grill at 250°F, season the pork shoulder generously with Pulled Pork Rub before placing it on the grill grate. After 1 hour of smoking, turn the pork and continue to smoke for another hour. In a broad cast-iron skillet, combine the onion with chicken stock. Place the pork in the skillet and cover the pork with aluminum foil after transferring it to the skillet. Cook for 2 hours, then raise the temperature to 300°F and cook for another hour.

2.While the pork is still on the grill, remove the lid and pull it with tongs. Because the stock will have decreased, mix the pork in the decreased, seasoned stock with the onions. Remove the out of the grill & set them aside, preheat a clean cast iron pan on medium-low flame. On the pan, melt the butter and oil, then toast the rolls by hand or with a metal spatula. Mix up the mustard & mayonnaise, then distribute it on both sides of the buns. Set them aside.

3.Place the pork, together with the sliced ham, on the pan in 4 portions. Cook for 2–3 minutes, turning the ham and pork halfway through. Pork, ham, pickles & cheese are layered one on top of the other. Allow 1 minute for the cheese to melt

4.Return the rolls to the pan, split each filled piece in half, and stack two rolls each prepared bun. Using the base of a metal spatula, press each sandwich down. Flip carefully and press down once more, remove the sandwiches off the pan and keep them warm until ready to serve.

NACHOS WITH PULLED PORK

Prep T: 30 mins /**Cook T:** 10 mins /**Serves:** 6

Ingredients:
- 1/2 diced avocado
- 1 cup of grated marble jack
- 1/4 cup of crema
- 2 lbs. of pork shoulder
- 1 teaspoon of red chili flakes
- 2 tablespoons of chopped scallions
- 1/4 cup of chopped red bell pepper
- 1/2 cup of apple cider
- 2 tablespoons of chopped jalapeno
- 1 cup of crumbled fresco
- 10 oz. of tortilla chips
- 2 tablespoons of chopped cilantro
- 2 tablespoons of chopped red onion
- 2 tablespoons of sweet heat rub
- 1 cup of water
- 2 tablespoons of chopped red onion

Directions:

1.Start your pellet grill and preheat at 225°F, combine Sweet Heat with chili flakes, then massage all sides of the pork shoulder with the mixture. Place the seasoned pork shoulder fat side up on the grill grate, shut the lid, and smoke the pork for approximately 2 12 hours, or till it achieves an internal temperature of 175°F.

2.Now, combine the pork, water, and cider in a disposable aluminum pan. Cook for another 2 hours, or till the pork achieves an internal temperature of 202° F, covered with aluminum foil. Allow the pork shoulder to rest for around 30 minutes before chopping with meat claws. Build two layers of toppings in a cast-iron pan, starting with chips and moving on to cheese, red onion, jalapeño, scallions, bell pepper, and cilantro.

3.Grill for around 10 minutes or until the cheese has melted. Avocado and crema go on top of the nachos. Serve immediately.

ASPARAGUS WRAPPED IN BACON

Prep T: 10 mins /**Cook T:** 25 mins /**Serves:** 4

Ingredients:
- 1 package of bacon
- 1 bunch of asparagus

Directions:

1.Preheat the grill to 400°F, one slice of bacon should be placed on a clean countertop, begin rolling the bacon all around 1 piece of asparagus from the bottom up. Rep with the remaining bacon bits.

2.Grill the asparagus wrapped in bacon for around 25 minutes, or till the bacon is crispy. To ensure that bacon cooks evenly, rotate the asparagus. Serve immediately.

BEER BRAISED GRILLED PORK BELLY

Prep T: 10 mins /**Cook T**: 12 h /**Serves**: 4
Ingredients:
- 3 cups of beef broth
- 2 cloves of garlic smashed
- 2 pounds of pork belly, chopped in 1-inch pieces
- 1 tablespoon of Chinese cooking wine
- 2 tablespoons of low sodium dark soy sauce
- 1 sliced onion
- 1 dark beer of any brand
- 3 tablespoons of sugar
- 1 teaspoon of Chinese five-spice powder
- 2 tablespoons of rice wine vinegar
- 1 inch of peeled and thinly sliced knob ginger

Directions:
1.Put a large Dutch oven on the medium-high flame on the stovetop—Brown the pork belly on all sides for around 5 minutes. Add the onion, garlic, & ginger after the pork belly has colored, and stir thoroughly.
2.Combine the soy sauce, beer, beef broth, sugar, rice wine vinegar, dark soy sauce, Chinese cooking wine, & Chinese five-spice powder. Bring the pan to boil with the cover on. Remove it out of the flame after it has reached a boil.
3.Preheat your Grill to 325°F. Put the pork belly pan on the grill & cook for around 12 hours, or till it is falling apart succulent & glazed. Take the pork belly out of the grill & serve right away.

PORK CHOPS STUFFED WITH CHEESY POTATOES

Prep T: 30 mins /**Cook T**: 30 mins /**Serves**: 4
Ingredients:
- 1 cup of cheddar cheese shredded
- 1 package of shredded frozen hash browns, thawed
- Pulled pork seasoning
- Diced white onion
- 4 pork chops bone-in
- 1/4 cup of sour cream
- 1 tablespoon of minced fresh parsley

Directions:
1.Put the pork chops on a work surface that is flat. Slice a pocket into the underside of each pork chop with a sharp knife, taking care not to break all the way via the chop. Pulled Pork Seasoning should be thoroughly applied on both sides of the pork chops.
2.Combine the hash browns, shredded cheddar, sour cream, parsley, chopped onion, and 1 tablespoon of Pulled Pork spice in a large-sized mixing dish. Using approximately a quarter cup of potato filling, stuff each pork chop. If necessary, secure the chop with a toothpick.
3.Preheat your grill at 350°F. Place the meat on the grill after inserting a temperature probe into the deepest section of one of the chops. Cook the chops for 10-15 minutes on one side, then turn and grill for yet another 10-15 minutes, or till the internal temperature reaches 145°F. Take the chops off the grill, remove the toothpicks from the meat, & serve right away.

KOREAN PULLED PORK

Prep T: 20 mins /**Cook T**: 16 h 30 mins /**Serves**:12
Ingredients:
The Meat:
- 1 boneless pork shoulder (8-lb, 3.6-kgs)

The Seasoning:
- ¾ cup of soy sauce
- 1/3 cup hoisin sauce
- 1/3 cup gochujang
- ¼ cup rice vinegar
- 1/3 cup tomato ketchup
- ¼ cup toasted sesame oil
- 3 tbsp. honey
- ½ tsp. black pepper
- 1 tbsp. Chinese five-spice
- 6 garlic cloves (peeled, chopped)
- ¼ cup fresh ginger (peeled and chopped)

The Sauce:
- 1 tbsp. canola oil
- ½ cup diced onion
- 1 cup chicken stock
- 2 tbsp. gochujang
- ½ cup tomato ketchup
- 2 tbsp. soy sauce
- 2 tbsp. honey
- 1½ tsp. Chinese five-spice powder
- 2 tsp. toasted sesame oil
- 2 tbsp. rice vinegar

Directions:
1.Preheat your grill to 240°F with the lid closed for between 12-15 minutes, first, prepare the seasoning. In a bowl, combine the soy sauce, hoisin sauce, gochujang, rice vinegar, tomato ketchup, sesame oil, honey, black pepper, 5-spice, garlic ginger.
2.Add the seasoning to a large Ziploc bag along with the pork shoulder. Seal the bag and massage gently to coat in the marinade evenly. Chill overnight, take the marinated pork out of the bag and place it directly on the grill.
3.Smoke for 8-10 hours until the meat registers an internal temperature of 195°F (90°C). Take the pork off the grill and transfer it to a baking pan. Cover loosely with aluminum foil and allow to rest for 10 minutes. In the meantime, prepare the BBQ sauce. Warm the canola oil in a saucepan over moderate heat. Add the onion and sauté until softened.
4.Next, stir in the chicken stock, gochujang, tomato ketchup, soy sauce, honey, and Chinese five-spice. Cook for 8-10 minutes until the sauce has reduced a little. Take off the heat and then stir in the sesame oil and vinegar.
Shred the cooked pork and serve with the BBQ sauce.

OVERNIGHT TAMARIND SPARE RIBS

Prep T: 20 mins /**Cook T**: 15 h 30 mins /**Serves**: 8
Ingredients:
The Meat:
- 2 racks fresh pork spare ribs, membranes removed

The Slather:
- 3 tbsp. Tamarind juice concentrate
- 1 tbsp. Honey
- 1 tbsp. Apple cider vinegar

The Rub:
- 3 tbsp. Light brown sugar
- 3 tbsp. Freshly ground black pepper
- 2 tbsp. Kosher salt
- 1 tbsp. Garlic powder
- 1 tbsp. Onion powder

The Soda Mop:
- ½ cup Cola, any brand
- ¼ cup Apple cider vinegar

The Smoke:
When you are ready to cook, preheat a smoker to 225°F (107°C) Alder wood chips work well with this recipe

Directions:
1.First, make the slather. Stir together the tamarind juice concentrate, honey, and apple cider vinegar in a small bowl. Brush the ribs all over with a thick layer of slather, removing any excess. Prepare the rub: combine the brown sugar, black pepper, salt, garlic powder, and onion powder in a small bowl. Coat the wet ribs with the dry rub, patting to create a crust. Cover and allow to rest overnight.

3.The following day, place the ribs, bone-side facing downwards, and smoke. Create a mop by combining the cola and apple cider vinegar in a bowl. You will need to apply the mop every 7-8 hours, or until the meat registers 165°F (74°C) and falls easily apart. Cover with foil and allow to rest for 20 minutes before serving. Serve and enjoy.

PORK CHOPS WITH GRILLED MANGO PINEAPPLE SALSA

Prep T: 10 mins /**Cook T:** 1 h 10 mins /**Serves:** 4

Ingredients:

The Meat:

- 3 (1-lb, 454-gms) thick-cut, bone-in pork chops

The Seasoning:

- 2 tbsp. Pork rub
- ¼ cup BBQ sauce, of choice

The Salsa:

- ½ pineapple (peeled, cored, diced)
- 1 ripe mango (peeled and diced)
- ½ red onion (peeled, sliced)
- 2 red bell pepper (deseeded, diced)
- 2 tbsp. fresh cilantro (chopped)
- 1 garlic cloves (peeled, minced)
- Juice of 1 medium lime
- Salt and black pepper

The Grill:

Preheat your grill to 450°F (232°C) with the lid closed for between 12-15 minutes, we recommend Applewood for this recipe

Directions:

1.Season the pork chops all over with the pork rub. Chill for half an hour, in the meantime, prepare the salsa. Combine the pineapple, mango, onion, bell pepper, cilantro, garlic, lime juice, salt, and black pepper. Set aside until ready to serve.

2.Place the chops on the preheated grill and cook for 8-9 minutes. Flip and brush the exposed side generously with BBQ sauce. Cook for another 8-9 minutes or until the meat registers an internal temperature of 165°F, allow the chops to rest for a few minutes before serving with the salsa.

MEDITERRANEAN MEATBALLS IN SPICY TOMATO SAUCE

Prep T: 20 mins /**Cook T:** 1 h 50 mins /**Serves:** 6
Ingredients:
The Meat:
- 1-lbs, 0.45-kgs Ground pork
- 0.5-lbs, 0.23-kgs Ground chorizo

The Meatballs:
- ¼ cup milk
- 2 medium-size eggs, beaten
- 1 tbsp. fresh garlic, minced
- 2 tbsp. yellow onion, minced
- 1 cup breadcrumbs
- 2 tsp. paprika
- 2 tbsp. fresh Italian parsley, finely chopped
- 2 tbsp. parmesan cheese, freshly grated + additional

The Sauce:
- 1 tbsp. olive oil
- ½ yellow onion, peeled and diced
- 2 tbsp. fresh garlic, minced
- 2-lbs, 0.9-kgs Canned diced tomatoes
- 2 tbsp. jarred piquillo peppers, diced
- 2 tbsp. granulated sugar
- 2 tsp. paprika
- 1 tsp. salt
- ½ tsp. chipotle chili powder
- 2 tbsp. green onions, chopped

The Smoke:
Preheat your smoker to 300° F (105°C) Use your favorite wood pellets for this recipe

Directions:
1.In a small-size bowl, whisk the milk with the eggs. Put to one side. In a second, larger mixing bowl, using clean hands, combine the ground pork with the ground chorizo. Add the garlic, onion, breadcrumbs, paprika, parsley, and two tablespoons of freshly grated Parmesan.

2.Add the milk-egg mixture to the meat mixture and incorporate. Roll the mixture into small evenly-sized meatballs, arrange the meatballs in a single layer on the smoker grid and cook for approximately 60 minutes. You will need to rotate the meatballs halfway through cooking. The meat is sufficiently cooked when it registers 160°F.

3.While the meatballs are cooking, prepare the tomato sauce, in a pan over medium heat, add the olive oil. When the oil is hot, add the onion and sauté for 2-3 minutes, until softened. Next, add the garlic and sauté until golden, for 2-3 minutes, pour in the canned tomatoes, and add the diced peppers, sugar, paprika, salt, and chipotle powder. Bring to a simmer for 20 minutes.

4.Using a handheld stick blender, blitz the tomato-chipotle mixture until almost smooth, with some small-size chunks remaining. When the meatballs have smoked for 60 minutes, transfer them to a disposable aluminum tray. Pour the tomato sauce over the top of the meatballs, and smoke for an additional 20 minutes. When you are ready to serve, remove from the smoker, garnish with more grated Parmesan cheese and serve.

SMOKED PORK SAUSAGE WITH BISCUITS AND GRAVY

Prep T: 20 mins /**Cook T**: 1 h 25 mins /**Serves**: 3

Ingredients:

The Meat:

- 12-ozs, 28.35-gms Tube pork sausage, casings removed

The Biscuits:

- 2 cups Flour
- ½ tsp. Salt
- 3 tsp. Baking powder
- ½ cup Butter, cold and cubed
- ¾ cup Whole milk

The Gravy:

- 2 tbsp. Flour
- 2 cups Whole milk
- Black pepper

The Smoke:

When you are ready to beginning cooking, with the lid open, set your pellet grill to 'smoke' and establish the fire; for 5 minutes Use mesquite wood pellets

Directions:

1.Place the pork sausage on the preheated grill and smoke for 30 minutes to one hour. In the meantime, make the biscuits. Cover a baking sheet with parchment paper and set it to one side. Combine the flour, salt, and baking powder, in a bowl. Cut in the butter cubes until the mixture is bread crumbs. Incorporate the milk gradually until the mixture forms a firm dough.

2.Lightly flour your worktop. Tip the dough out onto the worktop and knead until the dough comes together and is smooth. Gently shape the dough into a ½ -inch (1.25-cms) thick disc. Using round biscuit cutters, cut discs out of the dough. Place the discs on the baking sheet.

3.Take the cooked sausage off the grill and turn to 'grill.' Set the temperature to 450°F (232°C), close the lid, and allow it to come to heat.

4.Place the baking sheet of biscuits on the grill and cook for 10-12 minutes until risen and pale golden. In a skillet over moderately high heat, sauté the sausage for several minutes until browned and cooked through. Take the link out of the skillet and set it aside in a bowl. Do not drain the fat from the skillet.

5.Add the flour to the skillet and whisk to combine it with the fat— Cook for 60 seconds before whisking in the milk. Bring the mixture to a boil, then turn down to a simmer—Cook for a couple of minutes before returning the sausage to the skillet. Season to taste with black pepper, slice the cooked biscuits in half and top with the sausage gravy. Serve!

BEEF RECIPES

SMOKED ROAST BEEF

Prep T: 10 mins /**Cook T:** 12 to 14 h mins /**Serves:** 8
Ingredients:
- 1 (4-pound) top round roast
- 1 batch Espresso Brisket Rub
- 1 tablespoon butter

Directions:
1.Supply your smoker with wood pellets and follow the manufacturer's specific start-up procedure. With the lid closed, let the grill heat to 180°F. Season the top round roast with the rub. With the use of your hands, put the rub on the meat, place the roast directly on the grill grate and smoke until its internal temperature reaches 140°F. Take the roast off the grill.
2.Place a cast-iron skillet on the grill grate and increase the grill's temperature to 450°F. Place the roast in the skillet, add the butter, and cook until its internal temperature reaches 145°F. Flipping once after about 3 minutes. Take the roast off the grill and leave it within 10 to 15 minutes, before slicing and serving.

SMOKED BURGERS

Prep T: 15 mins /**Cook T:** 45 mins /**Serves:** 4
Ingredients:
- 1 pound ground beef
- 1 egg
- Wood-Fired Burger Shake, for seasoning

Directions:
1.Supply your smoker with wood pellets and follow the manufacturer's specific start-up procedure. With the lid closed, let the grill heat to 180°F. In a medium bowl, thoroughly mix the ground beef and egg. Divide the meat into 4 portions and shape each into a patty. Season the patties with the burger shake.
2.Place the burgers directly on the grill grate and smoke for 30 minutes. Increase the grill's temperature to 400°F and continue to cook the burgers until their internal temperature reaches 145°F. Take the burgers off the grill and serve as you like.

SMOKED BEEF RIBS

Prep T: 25 mins /**Cook T:** 4 to 6 h /**Serves:** 4 to 8
Ingredients:
- 2 (2- or 3-pound) racks beef ribs
- 2 tablespoons yellow mustard
- 1 batch Sweet and Spicy Cinnamon Rub

Directions:
1.Supply your smoker with wood pellets and follow the manufacturer's specific start-up procedure. With the lid closed, let the grill heat to 225°F.
2.Remove the membrane from the backside of the ribs. This can be done by cutting just through the membrane in an X pattern and working a paper towel between the membrane and the ribs to pull it off.
3.Coat the ribs all over with mustard and season them with the rub. With the use of your hands, put the rub on the meat. Place the ribs directly on the grill grate and smoke until their internal temperature reaches between 190°F and 200°F. Remove the racks from the grill and cut them into individual ribs. Serve immediately.

PELLET GRILL MEATLOAF

Prep T: 30 mins /**Cook T**: 6 h /**Serves**: 8

Ingredients:
- 1 cup breadcrumbs
- 2 pounds ground beef
- ¼ pound ground sausage
- 2 large eggs (beaten)
- 2 garlic cloves (grated)
- ½ teaspoon ground black pepper
- ¼ teaspoon red pepper flakes
- ½ teaspoon salt or to taste
- 1 teaspoon dried parsley
- 1 green onion (chopped)
- 1 teaspoon paprika
- ½ teaspoon Italian seasoning
- 1 small onion (chopped)
- 1 cup milk
- 1 cup BBQ sauce
- ½ cup apple juice

Directions:

1.Preheat the grill to 225°F with the lid closed for 15 minutes, using an apple pellet, in a large mixing bowl, combine the egg, milk, parsley, onion, green onion, paprika, Italian seasoning, breadcrumbs, ground beef, ground sausage, salt, pepper flakes, black pepper, and garlic. Mix thoroughly until the ingredients are well combined.

2.Form the mixture into a loaf and wrap the loaf loosely in tin foil and use a knife to poke some holes in the foil. The holes will allow the smoke flavor to enter the loaf, place the wrapped loaf on the grill grate and grill for 1 hour 30 minutes. Meanwhile, combine the BBQ sauce and apple juice in a mixing bowl.

3.Tear off the top half of the tin foil to apply the glaze. Apply the glaze over the meatloaf. Continue grilling until the internal temperature of the meatloaf is 160°F. Remove the meatloaf from the grill and let it sit for a few minutes to cool. Cut and serve.

BBQ BRISKET

Prep T: 30 mins /**Cook T:** 6 h /**Serves:** 8

Ingredients:

- 1 (12-14) packer beef brisket
- 1 teaspoon cayenne pepper
- 1 teaspoon cumin
- 2 tablespoons paprika
- 1 tablespoon smoked paprika
- 1 tablespoon onion powder
- ½ tablespoon maple sugar
- 2 teaspoon ground black pepper
- 2 teaspoon kosher salt

Directions:

1.Combine all the ingredients except the brisket in a mixing bowl. Season all sides of the brisket with the seasoning mixture as needed and wrap the brisket in plastic wrap. Refrigerate for 12 hours or more.

2.Unwrap the brisket and let it sit for about 2 hours or until the brisket is at room temperature. Preheat the pellet grill to 225°F with lid close, using mesquite or oak wood pellet. Place the brisket on the grill grate and grill for about 6 hours. Remove the brisket from the grill and wrap it with foil.

3.Return brisket to the grill and cook for about 4 hours or until the brisket's temperature reaches 204°F. Remove the brisket from the grill and let it sit for about 40 minutes to cool. Unwrap the brisket and cut it into slices.

TRI-TIP ROAST

Prep T: 30 mins /**Cook T:** 50 mins /**Serves:** 8

Ingredients:

- 2 pounds tri-tip roast (silver skin and fat cap removed)
- 1 teaspoon salt
- 1 teaspoon ground black pepper
- ½ teaspoon paprika
- 1 teaspoon fresh rosemary
- 1 teaspoon garlic powder
- 1 tablespoon olive oil

Directions:

1.Combine salt, pepper, garlic, paprika, and rosemary, brush the tri-tip generously with olive oil. Season the roast with seasoning mixture generously. Preheat the grill smoker 225°F with the lid closed for 15 minutes, using hickory, mesquite, or oak wood pellet. Place the tri-tip roast on the grill grate directly and cook for about 1 hour or until the tri tip's temperature reaches 135°F.

2.Remove the tri-tip from the grill and wrap it with heavy-duty foil. Set aside in a cooler. Adjust the grill temperature to high and preheat with lid closed for 15 minutes.

3.Remove the tri-tip from the foil and place it on the grill cook for 8 minutes, turning the tri-tip after the first 4 minutes, remove the tri-tip from the grill and let it rest for a few minutes to cool. Cut them into slices against the grain and serve.

FULLY LOADED BEEF NACHOS

Prep T: 10 mins /**Cook T**: 25 mins /**Serves**: 6
Ingredients:
- 1-lbs, 0.45-kgs Ground beef
- 1 large bag of tortilla chips
- 1 green bell pepper, seeded and diced
- ½ cup Scallions, sliced
- ½ cup Red onion, peeled and diced
- 3 cups Cheddar cheese, shredded
- Sour cream, guacamole, salsa – to serve

Directions:
1.In a cast-iron pan, arrange a double layer of tortilla chips. Scatter over the ground beef, bell pepper, scallions, red onion, and finally the Cheddar cheese.
2.Place the cast-iron pan on the grill and cook for approximately 10 minutes until the cheese has melted completely. Take off the grill and serve with sour cream, guacamole, and salsa on the side.

ITALIAN MEATBALLS

Prep T: 15 mins /**Cook T**: 120 mins /**Serves**: 4
Ingredients:
- 2 lb. beef
- 2 lb. pork
- 70-gram prosciutto
- 2 cups bread crumbs
- 1 tbsp. salt
- 1 tsp. fennel seed
- 2 tsp. oregano
- 2 cups whole milk ricotta
- 1 cup milk
- 2 eggs
- 2 tomatoes
- 1 tbsp. olive oil
- 1 cup basil leaves

Directions:
1.Prepare the Pit Boss grill, set the temperature to 375°F, and pre-heat with a closed lid. Combine pork, breadcrumbs, ground beef, and salt in a mixing bowl and mix with the help of hands. In another bowl, mix eggs, ricotta, and milk. Start adding the liquid mixture to the meat and keep mixing using hands; leave for 10 minutes once mixed perfectly.
2.Prepare a baking sheet with parchment paper lining, transform the meat mixture into meatballs and place it in the prepared baking sheet with proper spacing; there should be 48 meatballs, transfer the baking sheet to the pre-heated grill and cook for 15 to 20 minutes until meat is cooked through. Remove the baking sheet from the oven and reduce the temperature to 300F.
3.Once meatballs are cool, add crushed potatoes on top, apply some salt, shower three tablespoons of olive oil on top, cover with aluminum foil, and cook on the grill for an additional 80 to 90 minutes. Remove from grill, transfer to the serving dish and serve hot with basin garnish on top.

SWEET & SOUR BRISKET

Prep T: 15 mins /**Cook T**: 90 mins /**Serves**: 4

Ingredients:

- 1 kg brisket
- 1 kg Pit Boss prime rib rub
- 1 tbsp. salt
- 1 tbsp. butter
- 1 garlic, sliced
- 1 tsp. dried oregano
- 1 tsp. dried thyme
- 1 tsp. paprika
- 1 tsp. cayenne pepper
- 1 tsp. pepper
- 1 cup beef stock
- 1 cup ketchup
- 1 cup brown sugar

Directions:

1.Prepare the Pit Boss smoke grill, set the temperature to 375°F, and pre-heat. Place the brisket in a dish and season generously with kosher salt and Pit Boss Prime Rib Rub. Transfer the coated brisket on the grill directly with the fat side down and cook for 40 to 45 minutes until brisket changes colors to light brown.

2.Meanwhile, place a pan on the stove over medium heat, melt butter, add onion, cook for 4 to 6 minutes, and add garlic and sauté for one more minute. Then add cayenne, pepper, thyme, oregano, salt, and paprika, and cook for 30 seconds until aroma.

3.Pour beef stocking, frequently stir to scrap any ingredient on the bottom, add brown sugar and ketchup, and simmer for some time, remove the brisket from the grill, transfer it to a baking dish, reduce temperature to 225°F, add onion mixture and cover the dish with aluminum foil.

4.Remove from grill, exhaust the foil, let it cool down to room temperature, and transfer to the refrigerator for a night. Remove from refrigerator, set the grill temperature to 350F, and cook for 45 minutes until sauce caramelized. Remove from grill, transfer to the serving dish, slice, and serve with remaining sauce on top.

CHICKEN AND TURKEY RECIPES

CHICKEN BREASTS PELLET GRILL WITH FETA AND FRESH MINT

Prep T: 25 mins /**Cook T**: 15 mins /**Serves**: 4
Ingredients:
- 2 whole skinless, boneless chicken breasts 1piece (1½ ounces) feta cheese, thinly sliced
- 8 fresh mint leaves, rinsed, blotted dry, and cut into thin slivers Coarse salt (kosher or sea)
- Freshly ground black pepper
- tablespoon fresh lemon juice
- 1 tablespoon extra-virgin olive oil
- Wooden toothpicks
- Lemon wedges, for serving

Directions:
1.If using whole chicken breasts, cut each in half. Trim any sinews or excess fat off the chicken breasts and discard. Remove the tenders from the chicken breasts and set them aside. Place a half breast at the edge of a cutting board. Cut a deep horizontal pocket in the breast, taking care not to pierce the edges.
2.Repeat with the remaining breast halves. Place 2 or 3 slices of feta and a few slivers of mint in the pocket of each chicken breast. Pin the pockets shut with lightly oiled toothpicks. Place the breasts in a baking dish just large enough to hold them. Season the breasts on both sides with salt and pepper and sprinkle any remaining mint over them. 3.Drizzle the lemon juice and olive oil over both sides of the chicken breasts, patting them onto the meat with your fingers. Let the chicken breasts marinate in the refrigerator, covered, for 20 minutes, turning once or twice.
4.Turn the control knob to the high position, when the pellet grill is hot, place the chicken breasts on the pellet grill and cook for 10 to 14 minutes. Insert an instant-read meat thermometer into the thick part of a breast through one end: The internal temperature should be about 160°F.
5.Transfer the chicken breasts to a platter or plates and remove and discard the toothpicks. Serve the chicken at once with lemon wedges.

SALT-AND-PEPPER BONELESS CHICKEN

Prep T: 5 mins /**Cook T**: 15 mins /**Serves**: 4
Ingredients:
- 1½ pounds boneless, skinless, chicken breasts
- 2 tablespoons good-quality olive oil
- Salt and pepper

Directions:
1.Pat the chicken dry with paper towels, then pound to an even thickness if necessary. Brush with the oil and sprinkle with salt and pepper on both sides.
2.Turn the control knob to the high position, when the pellet grill is hot, place the chicken breasts and cook for 10 to 14 minutes. Transfer the chicken to a platter, let rest for 5 minutes, slice across the grain if you like, and serve.

CHICKEN SATAY WITH THAI PEANUT SAUCE

Prep T: 5 mins /**Cook T**: 8 mins /**Serves**: 4

Ingredients:

- 3 large boneless skinless chicken breasts or 6 boneless skinless thighs
- satay sticks
- Thai peanut sauce
- 1 cup creamy peanut butter
- ¾ cup coconut milk
- 1 Tbsp. soy sauce
- 1 Tbsp. fresh lime juice
- 1 Tbsp. brown sugar
- 2 Tbsp. sesame oil
- 2 tsp. crushed red pepper flakes
- 1 Tbsp. fish sauce
- 1 Tbsp. sriracha sauce
- 1 (3-in.) piece of ginger, peeled and diced
- 2 cloves garlic, minced
- ¼ cup chopped cilantro

Directions:

1.Cut chicken into 1.5-inch squares and place it onto satay sticks. Lightly season with salt. Combine all ingredients for sauce except the cilantro into a saucepan. Place saucepan over medium heat, mix ingredients using a whisk, and let simmer for 5 minutes.

2.Once ingredients have melded together, use either a blender or an immersion blender to blend until smooth. Pour into bowl and top with cilantro.

3.Turn the control knob to the high position, when the pellet grill is hot, place the chicken breasts and cook for 8 minutes. Because the chicken is cut into small pieces, it will cook rather quickly. But don't risk undercooked chicken. Ensure internal temperature meets minimum requirements of 165° Fahrenheit Remove from the pellet grill. Serve with sauce and cilantro.

CHICKEN SALAD WITH MANGO AND FRESH HERBS

Prep T: 10 mins /**Cook T**: 8 mins /**Serves**: 4
Ingredients:
- 1½ pounds boneless, skinless chicken breasts
- ¼ cup olive oil, plus more for brushing
- Salt and pepper
- Grated zest of 1 lime
- 2 tablespoons fresh lime juice
- 1 head Boston lettuce, torn into pieces
- ½ cup whole fresh mint leaves
- 1 ripe mango, peeled, pitted, and cut into 1-inch pieces

Directions:
1.Brush with oil and sprinkle with salt and pepper on both sides. Turn the control knob to the high position, when the pellet grill is hot, place the chicken on the pellet grill and cook for 8 minutes.
2.Transfer the chicken to a plate and let rest while you put the rest of the salad together. Make the dressing: Put the ¼ cup oil in a small bowl with the lime zest and juice and a pinch of salt. Whisk until the dressing thickens; taste and adjust the seasoning.
3.Put the lettuce and mint in a salad bowl and toss to mix. Cut the chicken across the grain into ½-inch slices and put over the greens. Top with the mango pieces, then drizzle with the dressing and serve (or toss before serving if you like).

SHEET PAN ROASTED CHICKEN

Prep T: 220 mins /**Cook T**: 40 mins /**Serves**: 2
Ingredients:
- 2 lb. chicken legs
- 2 tbsp. cilantro
- 2 tbsp. parsley
- 1 cup basil leaves
- 1 cup mint leaves
- 3 clove garlic
- 1 tsp. red pepper
- 1 tsp. salt
- 1 tbsp. lime juice
- 1 cup olive oil
- 2 carrots
- 1 onion

Directions:
1.Prepare the Pit Boss grill and pre-heat to 425F with a closed lid. Rinse the chicken and transfer it to a square bowl, combine parsley, garlic, cilantro, red pepper flake, mint, basil, lime juice, ½ cup of olive oil, put in the blender, and blend until mixture becomes smooth; put the puree over the chicken and make a good coating.
2.Transfer the chicken to the refrigerator and leave for 2 to 3 hours; put a small quantity of puree aside. Take the chicken out, clear the marinade coating, spread the chicken on the sheet tray, and put directly on the pre-heated grill; cook for 20 minutes until the chicken changes color to light brown.
3.Then add red onion, carrots, two tablespoon spoons of olive oil, pepper, and sale to the chicken and cook for an additional 15 to 20 minutes until internal temperature reaches 160F. Remove chicken from grill, leave to rest for 8 to 10 minutes, then serve with reserved marinade and fresh lime juice squeezed on top.

CHICKEN WITH ALABAMA SAUCE

Prep T: 70 mins /**Cook T**: 100 mins /**Serves**: 4
Ingredients:
- 3 lb. chicken
- 2 tbsp. Traeger chicken rub
- ¾ cup mayonnaise
- 3 tbsp. apple cider vinegar
- 3 tbsp. lemon juice
- 2 tbsp. apple juice
- 1 tbsp. garlic powder
- 1 tbsp. prepared horseradish
- 1 tbsp. black pepper
- 1 tsp. mustard powder
- 1 tsp. salt
- 1 tsp. cayenne pepper

Directions:
1.Prepare the Pit Boss smoke grill and pre-heat to 375°F with a closed lid. Place the whole chicken on the cutting board, remove the backbone and make two pieces of the whole chicken.
2.Then apply Traeger chicken rub on the inside of the chicken and set aside. In a small bowl, mix the white sauce with all other ingredients and set aside.
3.Place the chicken halves directly on the pre-heated grill and cook for 80 to 90 minutes until internal temperature reaches 160°F. Then remove chicken, apply white sauce mixture and transfer back to the grill; cook for another 8 to 10 minutes. Remove from grill, let it rest for some time, slice it and serve warm.

BAKED PROSCIUTTO-WRAPPED CHICKEN BREAST WITH SPINACH AND BOURSIN

Prep T: 3 h /**Cook T**: 30 mins /**Serves**: 4
Ingredients:
- 1 tbsp. Olive Oil
- Ten oz. Washed & Dried Baby Spinach Leaves
- 2 Whole Packs (5.2 Oz) Herbs Gournay Cheese & Boursin Garlic
- 2 lb. Boneless, Skinless Chicken Breasts
- Mrs. Dash Garlic & Herb Seasoning Blend
- 14 slices Prosciutto

Directions:
1.Heat the olive oil in a sauté pan. Cook for 3-5 mins, or unless the spinach has wilted. Using a filter, remov any excess liquid. Combine the spinach and cheese in a mixing bowl; after fully mixing, set aside.
2.Butterfly the chicken breast to open it like a book. Cover it with plastic wrap and use a meat mallet to lb i out finely. The chicken is additionally seasoned with Mrs. Dash spice.
3.A 2-foot-long sheet wrapping should be placed on a clean, flat surface. Prosciutto slices should be slightl overlapping and double-wide on the table. Place the chicken on top of the prosciutto, leaving a 1-inch borde all the way around.
4.The spinach mixture should be used to cover the chicken. Roll it up firmly to form a log. After tying th ends firmly, please place them in the refrigerator. Refrigerate for 2-3 hours, or overnight in the fridge.
5.Preheat the Traeger to 300°F with the lid closed for 12 mins when ready to cook.
6.Carefully remove the wrapper and place it straight on the grill plate. Bake for 1 hour and 15 mins, or unt the internal temperature reaches 162°F to 165°F. Remove the meat from the Traeger and set it aside for 1 mins before slicing.

CHICKEN ROAST WITH POTATOES

Prep T: 5 mins /**Cook T**: 70 mins /**Serves**: 4

Ingredients:

- 1 whole chicken
- 3 clove garlic minced
- 1 tbsp. salt
- 2 tbsp. pimento
- 2 tbsp. olive oil
- 3 tbsp. thyme
- 4 potatoes
- 1 tbsp. salt
- 1 tbsp. pepper
- 1 lemon
- 1 tbsp. parsley

Directions:

1.Prepare the Pit Boss smoke grill and pre-heat to 450F with a closed lid. Clean the chicken from the inside, rinse under freshwater, and pat dry with the help of a paper towel. Tie legs with kitchen twine and fold the wings behind the back.

2.Mix pimento, salt, and garlic in a small bowl, then add olive oil and apply the mixture completely on the outside of the chicken, place on the rimmed baking sheet, transfer to the refrigerator and leave for a night. Rinse the potatoes, scrub them, pour olive oil, apply pepper and salt and toss gently to make a coating of mixture on the potatoes, then spread in a roasting pan.

3.Remove chicken from refrigerator, place on the roasting pan on top of potatoes, pour freshly queezed lemon, and place potato rind on top. Transfer the roasting pan to the pre-heated grill and cook for 30 minutes; stir the potatoes frequently.

4.Reduce temperature to 350°F and cook for 40 more minutes until the internal temperature of the chicken reaches 165°F. Remove from grill, transfer the potatoes to the serving dish, place chicken on top, sprinkle lightly with pimentón, and serve with parsley on top.

ANCHO-CHILE SMOKED CHICKEN

Prep T: 5 mins /**Cook T**: 60 mins /**Serves**: 4
Ingredients:
- 1 tbsp. ancho chile powder
- 1 tbsp. brown sugar
- 1 tbsp. Espresso
- 1 tsp. cumin
- 1 tbsp. lime zest
- 1 tbsp. salt
- 3 tbsp. olive oil
- 1 tbsp. black pepper
- 8 chicken legs
- 4 tbsp. Traeger bbq sauce
- 1 lime
- 2 tbsp. parsley leaves

Directions:
1.Prepare the Pit Boss smoke grill and pre-heat to 180°F with a closed lid. Mix brown sugar, lime zest, ancho chile powder, salt, espresso, and cumin in a small dish. Place the chicken legs in the same dish, make an even coating of the spice mixture on the legs, cover the dish, and place in the refrigerator for a night.
2.Remove from fridge and place in the grill grate of pre-heated grill, cook for minutes. Then raise temperature to 350°F and cook for additional 60 minutes until internal temperature reaches 165°F.
3.Ten minutes before removing the chicken from the grill, apply bbq sauce with the help of a silicon brush. Finally, remove from grill, leave to rest for some time, then serve warm with fresh lime and parsley on top.

BBQ CHICKEN THIGHS

Prep T: 60 mins /**Cook T**: 150 mins /**Serves**: 4
Ingredients:
- 1 lb. each bone-in chicken thigh
- 1 cup chicken broth
- 4 tbsp. big game rub
- 1 cup butter
- 1 cup apricot bbq sauce

Directions:
1.Prepare the Pit Boss smoke grill and pre-heat to 250°F with a closed lid. Prepare the chicken thighs by removing skin and extra fat, then trim from top and bottom to make a uniform size of thighs. Cover the thighs with the skin, inject a tablespoon of chicken broth, and set aside for 50 to 60 minutes.
2.In the meantime, apply the Big Game Rub on the chicken thighs and transfer to the refrigerator, remove chicken thighs from the refrigerator, place on a large pan, pour melted butter, and place the pan on the pre heated grill grate. Cook the chicken for 60 minutes, then cover the pan with aluminum foil and cook for additional 60 minutes until internal temperature reaches 165F.
3.Then remove from grill, dip in the Apricot BBQ sauce, place on the clean pan and transfer to the grill again. Cook for another 15 to 20 minutes, remove from grill, let it rest for 8 to 10 minutes, and serve warm.

BACON WRAPPED CHICKEN

Prep T: 3 h /**Cook T**: 25 mins /**Serves**: 6
Ingredients:
- ½ cup ranch
- 1 tbsp. garlic powder
- 2 tbsp. chili sauce
- 1 tsp. oregano
- 302 g chicken breast
- 1 onion
- 2 green bell pepper
- 4 strips bacon

Directions:
1.Prepare the Pit Boss smoke grill and pre-heat to 425°F with a closed lid. Mix oregano, ranch, chile sauce, and garlic powder in a large bowl. Place diced chicken in the spice mixture and toss gently to make an even coating of slice on the chicken, transfer to the refrigerator and leave for 2 to 3 hours.
2.Thread a pepper, wedge of onion, chicken, and slice of bacon on the skewer, continue the process by alternating chicken and bacon in a manner that bacon wraps the chicken piece, do not overcrowd the skewer, continue the process with all the skewers.
3.Transfer the skewers to the pre-heated grill and cook each side for 5 minutes, a total of 20 minutes, until internal temperature reaches 165°F. Remove from grill, transfer to the serving plates and serve hot.

PRETZEL MUSTARD CHICKEN

Prep T: 5 mins /**Cook T**: 30 mins /**Serves**: 4
Ingredients:
- 1 lb. pretzel sticks
- 3 tbsp. Dijon mustard
- 3 tbsp. brown ale
- 1 tbsp. honey
- 2 tbsp. thyme
- 4 boneless chicken breast

Directions:
1.Prepare the Pit Boss smoke grill and pre-heat to 375°F with a closed lid, place the pretzel in a re-sealable plastic bag and crush with hands until it turns into a panko breadcrumbs-like texture, transfer to a shallow bowl. In another shallow bowl, mix cider, mustard, honey, and thyme.
2.Place the chicken in the mustard mixture, take it out, then place in the pretzel crumbs, and toss gently to make an even coating. Spray the grill grate with cooking spray. Transfer the coating chicken to the oiled grill grate and cook for 22 to 25 minutes until the internal temperature of the chicken reaches 165°F. Remove from grill, leave it to rest for 5 minutes, and serve with thyme garnish on top.

SEAFOOD RECIPES

SWEET SMOKED SHRIMPS GARLIC BUTTER

Prep T: 15 mins /**Cook T**: 20 mins /**Serves**: 10

Ingredients:

* 2-lbs., 0.9-kg. Fresh shrimps

The Rub:

* 2 tbsp. Lemon juice
* ½ tsp. Salt
* ½ tsp. Black pepper

The Glaze:

* 2 tbsp. Butter
* ½ tsp. Garlic powder

The Heat:

* Hickory wood pellets

Directions:

1.Peel the fresh shrimps and drizzle lemon juice over them. Let them rest for several minutes, after that, sprinkle salt and black pepper over the shrimps and spread them in a disposable aluminum pan.

2.Plug the wood pellet smoker and place the wood pellet inside the hopper. Turn the switch on, set the temperature to 200°F and prepare the wood pellet smoker for indirect heat. Wait until the wood pellet smoker is ready.

3.Insert the aluminum pan with shrimps into the wood pellet smoker and smoke the shrimps for approximately 20 minutes. Regularly check the shrimps and once they turn pink, take them out of the wood pellet smoker.

4.Add garlic powder to the butter, then mix until combined. The butter will be soft, baste the garlic butter over the smoked shrimps and serve. Enjoy!

GRILLED SWORDFISH

Prep T: 45 mins /**Cook T**: 20 mins /**Serves**: 4

Ingredients:

* 2 tbsp. olive oil
* 4 whole ear corns
* 1 tbsp. salt
* 1 tbsp. pepper
* 4 cherry tomatoes
* 2 tbsp. cilantro, chopped
* 1 red onion
* 1 serrano pepper minced
* 1 tbsp. lemon juice
* 4 whole swordfish fillets

Directions:

1.Set the Pit Boss grill temperature to 500°F and pre-heat with the lid closed. Place the corn in a dish, drizzle olive oil and sprinkle with pepper and salt.

2.Place the coated corn on the pre-heated grill and cook for 10 to 15 minutes until the color of the corn turns brown. Remove from grill, cut the kernels out and transfer to a bowl.

3.Then add red onion, lime juice, cilantro, tomatoes, and Serrano, mix well and sprinkle with pepper and salt.

4.Apply olive oil on the fish and sprinkle with pepper and salt, transfer to the grill and cook until fish becomes opaque and flakes come out quickly. It may take 15 to 18 minutes. Remove from grill, transfer to the serving dish and serve with corn salsa salad on top.

SWEET HONEY SOY SMOKED SALMON

Prep T: 2 h /**Cook T**: 2 h 10 mins /**Serves**: 10

Ingredients:

- 4-lbs., 1.8-kg. Salmon fillet

The Brine:

- ¾ cup Brown sugar
- 3 tbsp. Soy sauce
- 3 tsp. Kosher salt
- 3 cups Coldwater

The Glaze:

- 2 tbsp. Butter
- 2 tbsp. Brown sugar
- 2 tbsp. Olive oil
- 2 tbsp. Honey
- 1 tbsp. Soy sauce

The Heat:

- Alder wood pellets

Directions:

1.Add brown sugar, soy sauce, and kosher salt to the cold water, then stir until dissolved. Put the salmon fillet into the brine mixture and soak it for at least 2 hours. After 2 hours, take the salmon fillet out of the brine, then wash and rinse it. Plug the wood pellet smoker and place the wood pellet inside the hopper. Turn the switch on.

2.Set the temperature to 225°F and prepare the wood pellet smoker for indirect heat. Wait until the wood pellet smoker is ready. Place the salmon fillet in the wood pellet smoker and smoke it for 2 hours. In the meantime, melt the butter over low heat, then mix it with brown sugar, olive oil, honey, and soy sauce. Mix well.

3.After an hour of smoking, baste the glaze mixture over the salmon fillet and repeat it once every 1 minutes. Smoke until the salmon is flaky and remove it from the wood pellet smoker. Transfer the smoked salmon fillet to a serving dish and baste the remaining glaze mixture over it, serve and enjoy.

CRANBERRY LEMON SMOKED MACKEREL

Prep T: 2 h /**Cook T**: 2 h 10 mins /**Serves**: 10

Ingredients:
- 3.5-lb., 2.3-kg. Mackerel fillet

The Brine:
- 3 cans cranberry juice
- ½ cup pineapple juice
- 3 cups cold water
- ¼ cup brown sugar
- 2 cinnamon stick
- 2 fresh lemons
- 2 bay leaves
- 3 fresh thyme leaves

The Rub:
- ¾ tsp. kosher salt
- ¾ tsp. pepper

The Heat:
- Alder wood pellets

Directions:

1.Mix the cranberry juice and pineapple juice with water, then stir well. Stir in brown sugar to the liquid mixture, then mix until dissolved. Cut the lemons into slices, then add them to the liquid mixture and cinnamon sticks, bay leaves, and fresh thyme leaves.

2.Put the mackerel fillet into the brine and soak it for at least 2 hours. Store it in the refrigerator to keep the mackerel fillet fresh. After 2 hours, remove the mackerel fillet from the refrigerator and take it out of the brine mixture.

3.Plug the wood pellet smoker and place the wood pellet inside the hopper. Turn the switch on, set the temperature to 225°F and prepare the wood pellet smoker for indirect heat. Wait until the wood pellet smoker is ready.

4.Sprinkle salt and pepper over the mackerel fillet, then place it in the wood pellet smoker, smoke the mackerel fillet for 2 hours or until it flakes and removes it from the wood pellet smoker. Transfer the smoked mackerel fillet to a serving dish and serve, Enjoy!

CITRUSY SMOKED TUNA BELLY WITH SESAME AROMA

Prep T: 15 mins /**Cook T**: 2 h 10 mins /**Serves**: 10
Ingredients:
- 4-lbs., 1.8-kg. Tuna belly

The Marinade:
- 3 tbsp. sesame oil
- ½ cup of soy sauce
- 2 tbsp. lemon juice
- ½ cup of orange juice
- 2 tbsp. chopped fresh parsley
- ½ tsp. oregano
- 1 tbsp. minced garlic
- 2 tbsp. brown sugar
- 1 tsp. kosher salt
- ½ tsp. pepper

The Glaze:
- 2 tbsp. maple syrup
- 1 tbsp. balsamic vinegar

The Heat:
- Mesquite wood pellets

Directions:
1.Combine sesame oil with soy sauce, lemon juice, and orange juice, then mix well. Add oregano, minced garlic, brown sugar, kosher salt, pepper, chopped parsley to the wet mixture, and then stir unt incorporated. Carefully apply the wet mixture over the tuna fillet and marinate it for 2 hours. Store it in th refrigerator to keep the tuna fresh. After 2 hours, remove the marinated tuna from the wood pellet smoke and thaw it at room temperature.

2.Plug the wood pellet smoker and place the wood pellet inside the hopper. Turn the switch on, set th temperature to 225°F and prepare the wood pellet smoker for indirect heat. Wait until the wood pelle smoker is ready. Place the marinated tuna fillet in the wood pellet smoker and smoke it until flaky. Once is done, remove the smoked tuna fillet from the wood pellet smoker and transfer it to a serving dish, mix th maple syrup with balsamic vinegar, then baste the mixture over the smoked tuna fillet, serve and enjoy.

SAVORY SMOKED TROUT WITH FENNEL AND BLACK PEPPER RUB

Prep T: 15 mins /**Cook T**: 2 h 10 mins /**Serves**: 10
Ingredients:
- 4,5-lb., 2.3-kg. Trout fillet

The Rub:
- 2 tbsp. lemon juice
- 3 tbsp. fennel seeds
- 1 ½ tbsp. ground coriander
- 1 tbsp. black pepper
- ½ tsp. chili powder
- 1 tsp. kosher salt
- 1 tsp. garlic powder

The Glaze:
- 3 tbsp. olive oil

The Heat:
- Mesquite wood pellets

Directions:
1.Drizzle lemon juice over the trout fillet and let it rest for approximately 10 minutes, in the meantime, combine the fennel seeds with coriander, black pepper, chili powder, salt, and garlic powder, then mix well. Rub the trout fillet with the spice mixture, then set aside.
2.Plug the wood pellet smoker and place the wood pellet inside the hopper. Turn the switch on, set the temperature to 225°F and prepare the wood pellet smoker for indirect heat. Wait until the wood pellet smoker is ready, place the seasoned trout fillet in the wood pellet smoker and smoke it for 2 hours. Baste olive oil over the trout fillet and repeat it once every 20 minutes.
4.Once the smoked trout flakes, remove it from the wood pellet smoker and transfer it to a serving dish, serve and enjoy.

SPICED SMOKED CRABS WITH LEMON GRASS

Prep T: 15 mins /**Cook T**: 20 mins /**Serves**: 10
Ingredients:
- 5-lb., 2.3-kg. Fresh crabs
The Rub:
- 2 tbsp. smoked paprika
- 1 tsp. kosher salt
- 2 tbsp. dried parsley
- 2 tbsp. dried thyme
- 1 tbsp. black pepper
- 1 tsp. cayenne pepper
- 1 tsp. allspice
- ½ tsp. ground ginger
- ½ tsp. cinnamon powder
- 2 lemongrass
The Heat:
- Hickory wood pellets
Directions:
1.Combine the smoked paprika, salt, parsley, thyme, black pepper, ground ginger, cinnamon powder, cayenne pepper, and allspice, then mix well. Arrange the crabs in a disposable aluminum pan, then sprinkle the spice mixture over them. Add lemongrasses on top, then cover the seasoned crabs with aluminum foil.
2.Plug the wood pellet smoker and place the wood pellet inside the hopper. Turn the switch on. Set the temperature to 200°F and prepare the wood pellet smoker for indirect heat. Wait until the wood pellet smoker is ready.
3.Insert the aluminum pan with crabs into the wood pellet smoker and smoke the crabs for 30 minutes. Once it is done, take the smoked crabs out of the wood pellet smoker and serve, enjoy!

SMOKED WHITE SALAD

Prep T: 15 mins /**Cook T**: 3 h /**Serves**: 4

Ingredients:

- 1 cup salt
- 1 cup brown sugar
- 3 cup cold water
- 1 cup vodka
- 1 whole white fish
- 4 tbsp. celery chopped
- 2 onion, chopped
- 1 tbsp. lemon juice
- 2 tbsp. dill, chopped
- 4 tbsp. mayonnaise
- 3 tbsp. sour cream
- 1 tsp. black pepper

Directions:

1.Set the Pit Boss grill temperature to 180°F and pre-heat with the lid closed. Mix water, brown sugar, vodka, and salt in a large shallow roasting pan. Place fish in the pan, cover, and transfer to the refrigerator for 10 to 12 hours. Remove the pan from the refrigerator, take out fish, shake off excess brine, rinse under cold water and pat dry with the help of a paper towel.

2.Shift the fish to the grill, close the lid, and smoke for 2 ½ to 3 hours until the internal temperature of the fish reaches 150°F and fish flakes easily with a fork. Remove from grill, rest, then wrap in a plastic piece and place in the refrigerator.

3.Take out of the refrigerator, transfer to the mixing bowl and flake the fish and remove any bone if found, then add mayonnaise, red onion, sour cream, dill, pepper, celery, and lemon juice, mix well with the help of a spatula. Place the lettuce leaves on the serving plates, put the salad on top and serve immediately.

TEQUILA ORANGE MARINADE SMOKED LOBSTER

Prep T: 15 mins /**Cook T:** 1 h 10 mins /**Serves:** 10
Ingredients:
- 5-lb., 2.3-kg. Fresh lobsters

The Marinade:
- ¼ cup Tequila
- 3 tbsp. Lemon juice
- 2 cups Orange juice
- ½ tsp. Grated lemon zest
- ½ tsp. Grated orange zest
- 1 tsp. Kosher salt
- ¼ tsp. Pepper

The Heat:
- Hickory wood pellets

Directions:
1.Mix the tequila with lemon juice and orange juice, then stir well. Add grated lemon zest, orange zest, salt and pepper to the liquid mixture, then stir until dissolved. Drizzle the mixture over the lobsters and marinate them for at least 2 hours. Store the marinated lobsters in the refrigerator to keep them fresh.
2.After 2 hours, take the marinated lobsters out of the refrigerator and thaw them at room temperature. Plug the wood pellet smoker and place the wood pellet inside the hopper. Turn the switch on, set the temperature to 200°F and prepare the wood pellet smoker for indirect heat. Wait until the wood pellet smoker is ready.
3.Arrange the marinated lobsters in the wood pellet smoker and smoke them for an hour or until the smoked lobsters' internal temperature reaches 145°F. Remove the smoked lobsters from the wood pellet smoker and transfer them to a serving dish, serve and enjoy.

TUNA NOODLE CASSEROLE

Prep T: 75 mins /**Cook T:** 20 mins /**Serves:** 4
Ingredients:
- 1 wheat pasta box
- 2 cup yogurt
- 1 cup almond milk
- 1 tsp. mustard
- 1 tsp. celery salt
- 1 cup mushrooms, sliced
- 1 cup peas
- 1 cup Colby cheese
- 1 cup Monterey cheese

Directions:
1.Set the Pit Boss grill temperature to 350F and pre-heat with the lid closed. Place a pot on the stove over medium heat, fill with water, add salt and bring to boil, add pasta and cook according to the directions on the package, drain water, and set aside.
2.In a bowl mix together, celery salt, yogurt, ground mustard, milk, add tuna, cooked pasta, mushrooms, and peas, finally, add cheese. Shift the mixture to the parchment-lined baking sheet and sprinkle the remaining cheese on top.
3.Place the baking dish on the grill and cook for 40 to 45 minutes until cooked through and cheese melts completely. Remove from grill, transfer to the serving dish and serve hot.

GRILLED SALMON BURGER

Prep T: 20 mins /**Cook T**: 20 mins /**Serves**: 4

Ingredients:

- 2 Whole scallions, minced
- 1 jalapeno pepper, minced
- 1 tsp. black pepper
- 1 tbsp. cilantro minced
- 2 lb. salmon, skin and bones
- 1 tsp. salt
- 2 garlic clove
- 1 tbsp. chicken rub
- 1 cup mayonnaise
- 4 tbsp. butter lettuce
- 1 pickles onion
- 3 tbsp. dill pickles
- 4 brioche buns

Directions:

1.Set the Pit Boss grill temperature to 225°F and pre-heat with the lid closed. Combine jalapeño, scallions, garlic, cilantro, pepper, Traeger Chicken Rub, and salt in a blender and blend until mixed thoroughly.

2.Place the salmon in the blender and blend 2 to 3 times, then remove from blender and transform into four patties of equal weight. Transfer the patties to the baking sheet and place them in the refrigerator for 12 to 15 minutes.

3.Remove the salmon patties from the refrigerator and place them directly on the pre-heated grill. Cook each side for 4 minutes. Mix chipotle, mayonnaise, lime juice, pepper, adobo sauce, salt, and refrigerate in a bowl.

4.To prepare the burger, place the salmon Pattie on the bun, then place lettuce, pickled red onion, followed by chipotle mayo and your favorite topping.

MANDARIN SALMON

Prep T: 15 mins /**Cook T**: 20 mins /**Serves**: 4

Ingredinets:

- 1 tbsp. lime juice
- 2 tsp. sesame oil
- 2 cup mandarin orange sauce
- 3 tbsp. soy sauce
- 4 tbsp. cilantro, minced
- 1 tbsp. black pepper
- 2 whole salmon side

Directions:

1.Set the Pit Boss grill temperature to 375F and pre-heat with the lid closed. Mix sesame oil, cilantro, black pepper, lime juice, and soy sauce in a small bowl to prepare a glaze. Place the salmon on the cutting board and cut to 4 fillets, apply glaze to the fillet and transfer directly to the pre-heated grill with the skin side facing grill grating.

2.Cook the fish until internal temperature reaches 155°F that may take 18 to 20 minutes, apply glaze again halfway through the cooking time. Remove the salmon from the grill, transfer to the serving dish and serve hot.

GRILLED FISH TACOS

Prep T: 30 mins /**Cook T:** 20 mins /**Serves:** 4

Ingredients:

- 2 lime
- 1 lb. halibut
- 3 tbsp. veggie rub
- 2 tsp. Dijon mustard
- 1 tsp. salt
- 1 tsp. black pepper
- 2 tbsp. olive oil
- 3 garlic cloves, minced
- cabbage, shredded
- 1 onion, diced
- 2 tbsp. cilantro leaves
- 3 pickled jalapeno slices
- 1 avocado
- 3 tbsp. sour cream
- 8 corn tortillas

Directions:

1.Set the Pit Boss grill temperature to 400°F and pre-heat with the lid closed. Squeeze one lime while placing the other lime on the cutting board and cut to wedges. Mix mustard, pepper, lime juice, and salt in bowl, gently add the oil while stirring, and add garlic. Take a re-sealable bag, transfer the fish to the bag pour the marinade, mix completely and transfer to the refrigerator for 60 minutes.

2.Remove from refrigerator, take the fish out of the bag, shake off excess marinade, pat dry with the help a paper towel, and season both sides generously with Veggie Rub.

3.Transfer the coated fish to the preheated grill and cook until the fish becomes opaque and flakes easi with a fork. Remove from grill, shift to the cutting board, and cut to small cubes. Meanwhile, put the tortil on the grill and warm for 4 to 5 minutes, transfer the tortillas, fish, and other add-ons to the serving dis and serve with lime wedges as garnish.

LAMB RECIPES

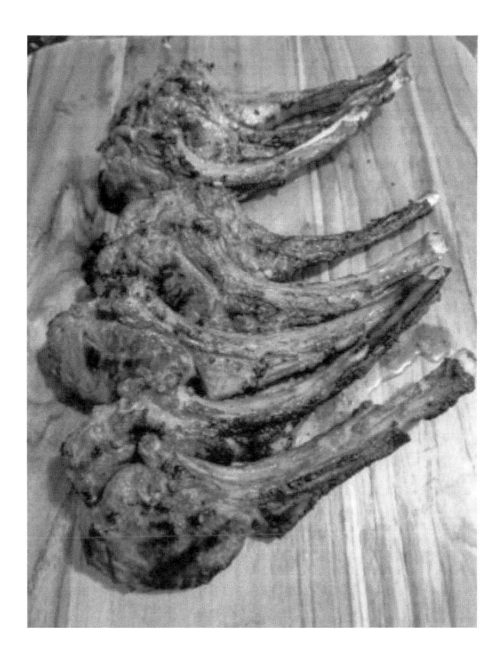

SEASONED LAMB SHOULDER

Prep T: 15 mins /**Cook T**: 5 h 30 mins /**Serves**: 6
Ingredients:
- 1 (5-pound) bone-in lamb shoulder, trimmed
- 3-4 tablespoons Moroccan seasoning
- 2 tablespoons olive oil
- 1 cup water
- ¼ cup apple cider vinegar

Directions:
1.Preheat the Pit Boss Grills Wood Pellet Grill & Smoker on the smoke setting to 275°F, using charcoal, coat the lamb shoulder with oil evenly and then rub with Moroccan seasoning generously. Place the lamb shoulder onto the grill and cook for about 45 minutes. In a food-safe spray bottle, mix vinegar and water.
2.Spray the lamb shoulder with vinegar mixture evenly, cook for about 4-5 hours, spraying with vinegar mixture after every 20 minutes.
3.Remove the lamb shoulder from the grill and place onto a cutting board for about 20 minutes before slicing, with a sharp knife, cut the lamb shoulder in desired-sized slices and serve.

LEMONY & SPICY LAMB SHOULDER

Prep T: 15 mins /**Cook T**: 2 h 30 mins /**Serves**: 8
Ingredients:
- 1 (5-pound) bone-in lamb shoulder, trimmed
- 2 tablespoons olive oil
- 1 tablespoon fresh lemon juice
- 1 tablespoon fresh ginger, peeled
- 4-6 garlic cloves, peeled
- ½ tablespoon ground cumin
- ½ tablespoon paprika
- ½ tablespoon ground turmeric
- ½ tablespoon ground allspice
- Salt and ground black pepper, as required

Directions:
1.Using a sharp knife, carve the skin of the lamb shoulder into a diamond pattern. Combine all the ingredients in a food processor and pulse until smooth. Coat the lamb shoulder with the pureed mixture generously.
2.Arrange the lamb shoulder into a large baking dish and refrigerate, covered overnight. Remove the baking dish of the shoulder from the refrigerator and set it aside at room temperature for at least 1 hour before cooking.
3.Preheat the Pit Boss Wood Pellet Grill & Smoker on grill setting to 225°F. Place the lamb shoulder onto the grill and cook for about 2½ hours.
4.Remove the lamb shoulder from the grill and place onto a cutting board for about 20 minutes before slicing. With a sharp knife, cut the lamb shoulder into desired-sized slices and serve.

SWEET & TANGY BRAISED LAMB SHANK

Prep T: 15 mins /**Cook T**: 10 h /**Serves**: 2
Ingredients:
- 1-2 cups water
- ¼ cup brown sugar
- 1/3 cup rice wine
- 1/3 cup soy sauce
- 1 tablespoon dark sesame oil
- 4 (1½x½-inch) orange zest strips
- 2 (3-inch long) cinnamon sticks
- 1½ teaspoons Chinese five-spice powder
- 2 (1¼-pound) lamb shanks

Directions:
1. Preheat the Pit Boss Wood Pellet Grill & Smoker on the smoke setting to 225-250°F, using charcoal and soaked applewood chips.
2. With a sharp knife, pierce each lamb shank at many places. In a bowl, add all remaining ingredients and mix until sugar is dissolved. In a large foil pan, place the lamb shanks and top with sugar mixture evenly.
3. Place the foil pan onto the grill and cook for about 8-10 hours, flipping after every 30 minutes. (If required, add enough water to keep the liquid ½-inch over). Remove from the grill and serve hot.

WOOD PELLET SMOKED LAMB SHOULDER

Prep T: 15 mins /**Cook T**: 1 h 30 mins /**Serves**: 6
Ingredients:
For Smoked Lamb Shoulder
- 5 lb. lamb shoulder, boneless and excess fat trimmed
- 2 tbsp kosher salt
- 2 tbsp black pepper
- 1 tbsp rosemary, dried
The Injection
- 1 cup apple cider vinegar
The Spritz
- 1 cup apple cider vinegar
- 1 cup apple juice

Directions:
1. Preheat the wood pellet smoker with a water pan to 2250°F. Rinse the lamb in cold water then pat it dry with a paper towel. Inject vinegar into the lamb.
2. Dry the lamb again and rub with oil, salt black pepper, and rosemary. Tie with kitchen twine, smoke uncovered for 1 hour then spritz after every 15 minutes until the internal temperature reaches 1950 F.
3. Remove the lamb from the grill and place it on a platter. Let cool before shredding it and enjoying it with your favorite side.

WOOD PELLET SMOKED PULLED LAMB SLIDERS

Prep T: 10 mins /**Cook T**: 7 h /**Serves**: 7
Ingredients:
- 5 lb. lamb shoulder, boneless
- ½ cup olive oil
- ¼ cup dry rub
- 10 oz spritz

The Dry Rub
- 1/3 cup kosher salt
- 1/3 cup pepper, ground
- 1-1/3 cup garlic, granulated

The Spritz
- 4 oz Worcestershire sauce
- 6 oz apple cider vinegar

Directions:
1.Preheat the wood pellet smoker with a water bath to 250°F, trim any fat from the lamb then rub with oil and dry rub. Place the lamb on the smoker for 90 minutes then spritz with a spray bottle every 30 minutes until the internal temperature reaches 165°F.
2.Transfer the lamb shoulder to a foil pan with the remaining spritz liquid and cover tightly with foil.
3.Place back in the smoker and smoke until the internal temperature reaches 200°F. Remove from the smoker and let rest for 30 minutes before pulling the lamb and serving with slaw, bun, or aioli. Enjoy.

WOOD PELLET SMOKED LEG OF LAMB

Prep T: 15 mins /**Cook T**: 3 h /**Serves**: 6
Ingredients:
- 1 leg lamb, boneless
- 4 garlic cloves, minced
- 2 tbsp salt
- 1 tbsp black pepper, freshly ground
- 2 tbsp oregano
- 1 tbsp thyme
- 2 tbsp olive oil

Directions:
1.Trim any excess fat from the lamb and tie the lamb using twine to form a nice roast. In a mixing bowl, mix garlic, spices, and oil. Rub all over the lamb, wrap with a plastic bag then refrigerate for an hour to marinate.
2.Place the lamb on a smoker set at 250oF. smoke the lamb for 4 hours or until the internal temperature reaches 145oF. Remove from the smoker and let rest to cool. Serve and enjoy.

SIMPLE GRILLED LAMB CHOPS

Prep T: 10 mins /**Cook T**: 6 mins /**Serves**: 6

Ingredients:
- 2 tbsp salt
- ½ tbsp black pepper
- 1 tbsp garlic, minced
- 1 onion, thinly sliced
- 2 tbsp olive oil
- 2 lb. lamb chops
- ¼ cup distilled white vinegar

Directions:

1.In a resealable bag, mix vinegar, salt, black pepper, garlic, sliced onion, and oil until all salt has dissolved, add the lamb chops and toss until well coated. Place in the fridge to marinate for 2 hours.

2.Preheat the wood pellet grill to high heat. Remove the lamb from the fridge and discard the marinade. Wrap any exposed bones with foil. Grill the lamb for 3 minutes per side. You can also broil in a broiler for more crispness. Serve and enjoy.

BRAISED LAMB SHANK

Prep T: 10 mins /**Cook T**: 4 h 30 mins /**Serves**: 4

Ingredients:
- 4 whole lamb shanks
- 2 tbsp. Traeger prime rib rub
- 1 cup beef both
- 1 cup red wine
- 3 tbsp. rosemary
- 3 tbsp. thyme

Directions:

1.Set Pit Boss grill temperature to 500°F and pre-heat with the lid closed. Place the lamb shank in a dish and generously apply Traeger Prime Rib Rub on all sides.

2.Transfer the lamb shanks to the pre-heated grill and cook for 20 minutes until external color changes to brown.

3.Remove from grill, transfer to the Dutch oven, add beef broth, herbs, and wine, cover tightly with lid and shift back to the grill, decrease the temperature to 325°F.

4.Cook for 3 ½ to 4 hours until the internal temperature of the shanks raises to 180°F. Remove from grill, transfer the lamb shank to the serving dish along with any juices and serve hot.

LAMB CHOPS WITH ROSEMARY

Prep T: 10 mins /**Cook T**: 10 mins /**Serves**: 4

Ingredients:

- 4 tbsp. olive oil
- 4 tbsp. onion, chopped
- 3 tbsp. shallot, chopped
- 2 garlic cloves, minced
- 2 tbsp. soy sauce
- 1 tbsp. balsamic vinegar
- 1 tbsp. sherry vinegar
- 2 tbsp. rosemary
- 2 tsp. Dijon mustard
- 2 tsp. Worcestershire sauce
- 1 tbsp. black pepper
- 3 lb. lamb chops

Directions:

1.Set Pit Boss grill temperature to 500°F and pre-heat with the lid closed. Place a pan on the stove over medium heat, add 1 tbsp. of olive oil until hot, and then add garlic and onion, sauté until onion turn translucent.

2.Shift to the food processor, add vinegar, mustard, Worcestershire sauce, soy sauce, rosemary, and process then sprinkle pepper and salt, slowly add the rest of the olive oil and keep blending until sauce become consistent and smooth, set aside.

3.Place the lamb chops in a dish, apply olive oil on all sides of the chops, and then sprinkle pepper and salt generously. Transfer the chops to the grill and cook each side for 5 to 6 minutes until the internal temperature of the chop reaches 135°F. Remove from grill, transfer to the serving plates and serve hot with rosemary sauce as dipping.

IRISH LAMB STEW

Prep T: 10 mins /**Cook T**: 7 h /**Serves**: 4

Ingredients:

- 4 lb. boneless lamb shoulder
- 1 tbsp. salt
- 1 tbsp. Pepper
- 2 tbsp. olive oil
- 3 tbsp. bacon, chopped
- 1 onion, chopped
- 2 garlic cloves, minced
- 1 cup white wine
- 3 cup beef stock
- 3 whole bay leaves
- 2 tbsp. rosemary
- 2 tbsp. thyme
- 2 large potatoes, diced
- 2 carrots
- 1 cup flour
- 1 cup butter

Directions:

1.Set Pit Boss grill temperature to 350°F and pre-heat with the lid closed. Place the lamb in a dish and season with pepper and salt. Place Dutch oven on a stove over medium heat, add olive oil until hot, then cook lamb in batches until brown and set aside.

2.Add bacon to Dutch oven and cook for 18 to 20 minutes, frequently stirring until color changes to light brown, shift bacon to the separate dish, and reserve 2 tbsp of bacon fat. Pour reserved bacon fat in the Dutch oven, add onions and sauté until transparent, add garlic and cook for additional 30 seconds.

3.Then add lamb and bacon back to the oven, deglaze with white wine and remove any bit from the bottom with the help of a wooden spoon.

4.Finally, add potatoes, herbs, stock, and carrots to the oven, bring to simmer, cover the oven and shift to the grill, and cook for 1 to 2 hours until lamb is soft. Remove the oven from the grill and transfer it back to the stove over medium heat. In a small bowl mix together, flour and butter, add to the stew, and cook for 8 to 10 more minutes until stew gets thicker. Remove from oven, sprinkle pepper and salt, and serve with rosemary and thyme garnishing.

ROASTED LAMB SHOULDER

Prep T: 10 mins /**Cook T**: 7 h /**Serves**: 4

Ingredients:
- 1 tbsp. caraway seeds
- 1 tsp. coriander seeds
- 1 tsp. cumin seeds
- 2 tbsp. ancho chilies
- 1 cup water
- 1 tsp. paprika
- 1 tbsp. lemon juice
- 2 garlic clove
- 3 tbsp. olive oil
- 1 tbsp. salt
- 1 tsp. mint leaves
- 2 tsp. lemon juice

Directions:

1.Set the Pit Boss grill temperature to 325°F and pre-heat with the lid closed. Add caraway, cumin seeds and coriander to the spice grinder and grind finely. Pour water in a microwave-safe bowl, add ancho chiles and microwave for 1 to 2 minutes, then remove and let it cool a bit, and then transfer 2 tbsp. of water and soft chiles to the blender.

2.Add lemon juice, olive oil, dried mint leaves, garlic cloves, paprika, ground spices, and salt, blend until harissa becomes consistent and smooth, place the lamb in a medium dish and apply half of the harissa, ru thoroughly and leave at room temperature for 1 to 2 hours, then pour half of the water in the dish, cover and cook for 2 to 2 ½ hours on the grill, add water when needed.

3.Then remove foil and cook for another 2 to 2 ½ hours until lamb is tender, remove from grill and let i rest for 15 to 20 minutes. At the same time, mix cilantro, olive oil, garlic clove, and yogurt in a small bow set aside. Pull the lamb off the bone with a fork, transform it into smaller pieces and serve with remainin harissa, yogurt sauce, and naan bread.

GRILLED LAMB BURGER

Prep T: 10 mins /**Cook T**: 7 h /**Serves**: 4

Ingredients:

- 2 lb. ground lamb
- 1 jalapeno pepper, minced
- 5 scallions, minced
- 2 tbsp. mint
- 3 tbsp. dill, minced
- 6 garlic cloves, minced
- 2 tbsp. salt
- 2 tbsp. black pepper
- 1 red bell pepper
- 1 cup mayonnaise
- 2 tsp. lemon juice
- 4 slices mango cheese
- 4 large brioche buns
- 1 cup arugula
- 1 tomato, sliced
- 1 onion, sliced

Directions:

1.Set the Pit Boss grill temperature to 500°F and pre-heat with the lid closed. Mix mint, pepper, garlic, scallions, lamb, salt, jalapeno, and dill in a mixing bowl, make four equal portions of the mixture and transform them into ¾ inch thick patties, set aside.

2.Put the red bell pepper on the grill for 20 minutes, keep rolling until charred completely, put in the re-sealable bag for 10 minutes, then remove from bag, cut to half, discard seeds and remove the skin.

3.In a food processor, add mayonnaise, garlic, pepper, roasted red pepper, salt, and lemon juice, process until mixture becomes consistent, set aside. Transfer the lamb burgers to the grill and cook each side for 4 to 5 minutes.

4.Also, place the buns on the grill to toast at the last cooking moments and add a slice of cheese on top of Pattie.

5.Assemble burgers by spreading mayo mixture on the bun, add lamb Pattie, top with onion, arugula, and tomato. Serve with favorite dipping and sides.

GRILLED LAMB CHOPS

Prep T: 10 mins /**Cook T:** 14 mins /**Serves:** 2

Ingredients:

- 4 lamb chops
- 1 cup extra virgin olive oil, divided
- 1/2 cup onion, coarsely chopped
- 5 cloves garlic, coarsely chopped
- 4 teaspoons of coconut amino
- 1 tablespoon sherry vinegar
- 1 teaspoon fresh rosemary needles
- 4 teaspoons Dijon mustard
- 1 teaspoon Worcestershire sauce
- Salt and black pepper, as needed

Directions:

1.Take a skillet, and add onion, and garlic along with one tablespoon of olive oil, and cook over medium hea until onions become translucent.

2.Transfer this mixture to the blender and add coconut amino, rosemary, vinegar, mustard, an Worcestershire sauce, next, add salt and black pepper. Now, pour the remaining olive oil, while the machin is running until the sauce is emulsified.

3.If the sauce is too sticky, you can add 2 tablespoons of water. Preheat the smoker grill for 15 minutes, a 225°F.

Generously brush the lamb chops on both sides with the olive oil and season with salt and black peppe place lamb chops directly on the grill grate and close the lid.

4.Grilled the lamb chops 7 minutes per side, or until the internal temperature reaches 135°F. Once done serve and enjoy with prepared blended sauce.

VEGGIE RECIPES

GRILLED CORN WITH HONEY AND BUTTER

Prep T: 30 mins /**Cook T**: 10 mins /**Serves**: 4

Ingredients:

- 6 pieces corn
- 2 tablespoons olive oil
- 1/2 cup butter
- 1/2 cup honey
- 1 tablespoon smoked salt
- Pepper to taste

Directions:

Preheat the wood pellet grill too high for 15 minutes while the lid is closed. Brush the corn with oil and butter, grill the corn for 10 minutes, turning from time to time. Mix honey and butter, brush corn with this mixture and sprinkle with smoked salt and pepper.

Pit Boss Grill Cookbook| Cole Palmer

GRILLED SWEET POTATO PLANKS

Prep T: 30 mins /**Cook T:** 30 mins /**Serves:** 8
Ingredients:
- 5 sweet potatoes, sliced into planks
- 1 tablespoon olive oil
- 1 teaspoon onion powder
- Salt and pepper to taste

Directions:
1.Set the Wood pellet grill too high, preheat it for 15 minutes while the lid is closed.
2.Coat the sweet potatoes with oil, sprinkle with onion powder, salt, and pepper. Grill the sweet potatoes for 15 minutes.

ROASTED VEGGIES AND HUMMUS

Prep T: 30 mins /**Cook T:** 20 mins /**Serves:** 4
Ingredients:
- 1 white onion, sliced into wedges
- 2 cups butternut squash
- 2 cups cauliflower, sliced into florets
- 1 cup mushroom buttons
- Olive oil
- Salt and pepper to taste
- Hummus

Directions:
1.Set the Wood pellet grill too high, preheat it for 10 minutes while the lid is closed.
2.Add the veggies to a baking pan, roast for 20 minutes. Serve roasted veggies with hummus.

GRILLED SPICY SWEET POTATOES

Prep T: 10 mins /**Cook T:** 35 mins /**Serves:** 6
Ingredients:
- 2 lb. sweet potatoes, cut into chunks
- 1 red onion, chopped
- 2 tbsp. oil
- 2 tbsp. orange juice
- 1 tbsp. roasted cinnamon
- 1 tbsp. salt
- ¼ tbsp. Chipotle chili pepper

Directions:
1.Preheat the wood pellet grill to 425°F with the lid closed. Toss the sweet potatoes with onion, oil, a juice.
2.In a mixing bowl, mix cinnamon, salt, and pepper, then sprinkle the mixture over the sweet potato spread the potatoes on a lined baking dish in a single layer. Place the baking dish in the grill and grill for minutes or until the sweet potatoes are tender, serve and enjoy.

GRILLED MEXICAN STREET CORN

Prep T: 5 mins /**Cook T**: 25 mins /**Serves**: 6
Ingredients:
- 6 ears of corn on the cob
- 1 tbsp. olive oil
- Kosher salt and pepper to taste
- ¼ cup mayo
- ¼ cup sour cream
- 1 tbsp. garlic paste
- ½ tbsp. chili powder
- Pinch of ground red pepper
- ½ cup coria cheese, crumbled
- ¼ cup cilantro, chopped
- 6 lime wedges

Directions:
1.Brush the corn with oil, sprinkle with salt. Place the corn on a wood pellet grill set at 350°F. Cook for 25 minutes as you turn it occasionally, mix mayo, cream, garlic, chili, and red pepper until well combined.
2.Let it rest for some minutes, then brush with the mayo mixture. Sprinkle cottage cheese, more chili powder, and cilantro. Serve with lime wedges. Enjoy.

PERFECTLY SMOKED ARTICHOKE HEARTS

Prep T: 10 mins /**Cook T**: 2 h /**Serves**: 10
Ingredients:
- 12 canned whole artichoke hearts
- ¼ cup of extra virgin olive oil
- 4 cloves of garlic minced
- 2 Tbsp. of fresh parsley finely chopped (leaves)
- 1 Tbsp. of fresh lemon juice freshly squeezed
- Salt to taste
- Lemon for garnish

Directions:
1.Start the pellet grill on smoke with the lid open until the fire is established. Set the temperature to 350 F and preheat, lid closed, for 10 to 15 minutes.
2.In a bowl, combine all remaining ingredients and pour over artichokes. Place artichokes on a grill rack and smoke for 2 hours or so. Serve hot with extra olive oil and lemon halves.

WOOD PELLET SMOKED MUSHROOMS

Prep T: 15 mins /**Cook T**: 45 mins /**Serves**: 2
Ingredients:
- 4 cups whole baby portobello, cleaned
- 1 tbsp canola oil
- 1 tbsp onion powder
- 1 tbsp garlic, granulated
- 1 tbsp salt
- 1 tbsp pepper

Directions:
1.Place all the ingredients in a bowl, mix, and combine, set your Wood pellet to 180°F. Place the mushrooms on the grill directly and smoke for about 30 minutes.
2.Increase heat to high and cook the mushroom for another 15 minutes. Serve warm and enjoy!

GRILLED GREENS AND CHEESE QUESADILLAS

Prep T: 20 mins /**Cook T**: 8 mins /**Serves**: 8
Ingredients:
- 2 tbsp. vegetable oil
- ½ medium white onion, finely chopped
- 2 finely grated garlic cloves
- 10 ounces' Swiss chard or chopped nettle
- 2 tsp. of fresh lime juice
- Kosher salt
- 6 ounces Toma cheese or grated sharp cheddar
- 8 corn tortillas
- Grilled Salsa Roja
- Avocado
- Tomatillo
- Salsa Verde

Directions:
1.Heat the oil in a big skillet. Cook the onion and garlic, turning as soon as in a while, for approximately 6 or 8 minutes. Add the greens, a group at a time. Pour in ½ cup water and cook, now and then turning, until greens are delicate, for approximately 6 or 8 minutes. Add the lime juice, then season with salt. Move onto a plate and let it cool.
2.Heat a skillet over medium heat and upload 2 tbsp of cheddar proper on it. Top with a tortilla and cook squeezing with a spatula, until cheddar is softened and crisp, around 1 minute. Put the cheddar facet up on a baking sheet.
3.Repeat with the other cheese and tortillas to make seven extra quesadillas, top every quesadilla with tbsp. Of veggies combination, fold them in half, and keep cooking, turning once, till the vegetables are hea and tortillas are toasted- around four minutes. Serve the quesadillas with Grilled Salsa Roja and Avocad Tomatillo Salsa Verde.

GRILLED CORN ON THE COB

Prep T: 20 mins /**Cook T**: 30 mins /**Serves**: 2
Ingredients:
- Corn on the cob, fresh
- Butter & salt for serving

Directions:
1.Preheat your pellet grill over excessive warmth in advance. Remove some outer layers of the corn husks.
2.Remove the top from every cob using scissors & trim any free husk leaves as well. Place the corn over th new grill (preferably in their husks) & close the lid. Cook for 25 to 30 minutes, till all sides of the husks, fli charred, turning after each eight to 10 mins.
3.Remove the corn from the grill. Let take a seat till you can easily cope with it, for a couple of minutes Remove the charred husks & silks from the corn. Apply some butter and salt on hot corn, rubbing it nicely Serve warm and enjoy.

DESSERTS

BROWNIE BREAD BAKED PUDDING

Prep T: 10 mins /**Cook T**: 45 mins /**Serves**: 6
Ingredients:
- 1/2 cup of bittersweet chocolate chips
- 2 sticks of butter
- 4 eggs
- 1 teaspoon of baking soda
- 3 teaspoons of vanilla extract
- 1 cup of heavy cream
- 1/4 candied walnuts
- 1 pinch of salt
- 1/4 cup of dried coconut flakes
- 1/2 teaspoon of salt
- 4 cups of Leftover brownies, cut into 1" cubes
- Whipped cream
- 1/2 cup of sugar
- 2 cups of brown sugar

Directions:
1.Preheat the pellet grill to 350°F and leave the lid closed for 15 minutes until ready to cook. To make the bread pudding, whisk together heavy cream, vanilla, sugar, eggs, and salt in a small-sized mixing dish. Whisk everything together well. Toss brownies & chocolate chips.

2.Fill an oiled 9x13 baking pan halfway with the mixture and sprinkle with coconut flakes. Cook for around 45 minutes, or until the sides are gently colored and puffed and the center is barely set, by placing the baking pan straight on the grill grate.

3.To make the caramel sauce, mix salt, butter, and sugar in a medium-sized saucepan on medium-high flame. Bring the mixture to a boil, then reduce to a low flame and continue to simmer till an instant-read thermometer registers 275°F.

4.Remove the pan from the flame and stir in the vanilla & baking soda. As it will bubble up & release steam, proceed with caution. Serve alongside caramel sauce, whipped cream, & candied walnuts on top of the brownie bread pudding. Enjoy!

CHERRY CRISP LAYERED WITH SWEET CREAM

Prep T: 20 mins /**Cook T**: 50 mins /**Serves**: 6

Ingredients:

For the cherry filling:
- 1/2 cup of dark brown sugar
- 1 tablespoon of corn-starch
- 4 cups of pitted frozen cherries
- 1 teaspoon of allspice
- 1 tablespoon of fresh lemon juice
- 2 tablespoons of all-purpose flour
- 1/2 cup of granulated sugar

For the crisp topping:
- 1/2 cup of all-purpose flour
- 1 teaspoon of ground cinnamon
- 1 1/2 cups of rolled oats
- 1 teaspoon of kosher salt
- 1 stick of butter salted, cut into small cubes
- 1/2 cup of dark brown sugar, packed
- 1 tablespoon of vanilla extract

For the sweet cream:
- 1/2 cup of granulated sugar
- 1 tablespoon of vanilla bean paste
- 1 cup of sour cream
- 1/2 cup of whole buttermilk

Directions:

1.Once ready to cook, preheat the pellet grill to 385°F for 15 minutes with the lid closed. Combine all of the components for the cherry filling in a medium-sized stainless steel mixing bowl.

2.Place the cast iron skillet with the cherry filling combination on the grill. Let the cherry filling mix come to room temperature before simmering, stirring periodically, for 15 to 20 minutes, or until the liquid has thickened.

3.To create the crisp topping, combine all of the ingredients in a separate dish and, using both hands, knead the butter into the flour and oats to produce a crumble-style topping. Set aside after thoroughly mixing.

4.Remove the cherry filling out from the grill with heatproof gloves and set it on a heat-safe surface. Return to the grill after topping with the crisp topping—Bake for an additional 10 to 15 minutes, or until the topping is done to your liking.

5.To make the sweet cream, whisk together all of the ingredients in a separate dish until thoroughly combined. Put it in the fridge to maintain it cold until you're ready to use it.

6.Allow for 15 minutes of resting time after removing the cast iron from the grill. Spoon & serve with a dollop of sweet cream on top. Enjoy!

GRILLED WATERMELON AND PINEAPPLE CREAM SICLES

Prep T: 10 mins /**Cook T**: 1 h 20 mins /**Serves**: 8
Ingredients:
- 1/2 trimmed and sliced whole pineapple
- 2 whole freshly squeezed lime juice
- 1/2 whole sliced watermelon
- 1 cup of heavy cream
- 1/2 cup of sugar

Directions:
1.When you're ready to cook, turn the pellet grill on Smoke and follow the instructions on the grill, cook for 15-20 minutes on the grill with the watermelon and pineapple. Remove the watermelon from the grill and remove the rind. Move to a blender after cutting into pieces.
2.Strain after pureeing until smooth. Continue with the pineapple, but keep them separate. Put 1/2 cup of sugar, 1/2 cup cream, and 1 lime juice to each juice. 4.Whisk until the sugar is completely dissolved. Fill each popsicle mold 1/4 full with pineapple, 1/2 full with watermelon, and 1/4 full with pineapple. Freeze the molds for 1 hour or until they are partially frozen.
3.Place the popsicle stick in the freezer overnight till it's well frozen. To remove the pop, pour hot water over the outside of the mold and peel it away carefully. Enjoy!

S'MORES SMOKED CAKE BARS

Prep T: 480 mins /**Cook T**: 50 mins /**Serves**: 8
Ingredients:
- 2 cups of graham cracker crumbs
- 1 stick of melted butter
- 1 1/2 cups of mini marshmallows
- 2 cups of chocolate chips
- 1 box of yellow cake mix
- 1 egg
- 7 oz. of marshmallow crème

Directions:
1.Preheat your pellet grill to 250° F by turning it on SMOKE mode and letting it run with the lid open for 10 minutes. Aluminum foil must be used to layer a 9x13" metal pan.
2.Combine the cake mix, butter, egg, and graham cracker crumbs in a large-sized mixing dish with a hand mixer. 2 cups of graham cracker mixture should be set aside, then spread the leftover graham cracker combination into the prepared pan.
3.Dollop the marshmallow crème over the chocolate chips, then distribute the chocolate chips on top. Sprinkle with tiny marshmallows after spreading into a uniform layer. Top with the graham cracker mixture that was set aside. Place on the grill for around 45 to 50 minutes to smoke. Before cutting into bars, allow it to cool fully.

GINGERBREAD BAKED COOKIES

Prep T: 15 mins /**Cook T**: 2h 30 mins /**Serves**: 8

Ingredients:

- 1/2 cup of whole wheat flour
○ 2 ounces of butter unsalted
- 1/2 teaspoon of ground cinnamon
- 1/8 teaspoon of ground cloves
- 3/4 cup of all-purpose flour
- 1 teaspoon of honey
- Powdered sugar
- 1 cup of cake flour
- 1 cup of granulated sugar
- 1 1/2 teaspoons of ginger
- 1/2 teaspoon of kosher salt
- 1/3 cup of brown sugar

Directions:

1.Combine flours, clove, cinnamon, ginger, and baking soda in a mixing dish. Toss in the salt and mix everything together. In a separate dish, with a fork, mix both sugars & honey.

2.In the dish of a stand mixer equipped with a paddle attachment, place the butter. Turn the mixer to medium-low and cream the butter till it is creamy. Mix in the sugar mixture for 2 minutes or until frothy.

3.Scrape down the bowl's edges and bottom. After each addition, Stir the dry ingredients in two batches, mixing at low speed just until combined. Scrape the inside of the dish.

4.Wrap the dough in plastic wrap and form a block. Wrap the dough in plastic wrap and place it in the refrigerator for around 2 hours or overnight. Roll out the dough to a thickness of 1/8 inch. Cut cookies with a cookie cutter.

5.Start the pellet grill on Smoke with the lid open till the fire is formed when you're ready to cook (4 to 5 minutes)—Preheat at 325°F with the lid covered for around 10 to 15 minutes.

6.In the grill, bake the cookies for around 13 to 15 minutes on a baking sheet coated with parchment paper. Just before serving, dust with powdered sugar. Enjoy!

BUTTERMILK PIE BAKED WITH CORNMEAL CRUST

Prep T: 30 mins /**Cook T**: 1 h 45 mins /**Serves**: 8

Ingredients:
- 8 tablespoons of unsalted butter
- 1/4 cup of flour
- 2 teaspoons of fresh lemon juice
- 1 cup of all-purpose flour
- 1/4 cup of ice water
- 3/4 cup of buttermilk
- 1 teaspoon of kosher salt
- 1/3 cup of cornmeal
- 3 whole eggs
- 1/4 teaspoon of lemon zest
- 1 1/2 cups of sugar
- 1 whole vanilla bean, split & scraped
- 1/4 cup of Crisco

Directions:

1.Preheat the pellet grill to 350°F and cook for 15 minutes with the lid covered. Before you begin, chill all o the crust ingredients.

2.To make the crust, put cornmeal, flour, and salt in a food processor and process 3 times to incorporate Pulse 3 to 3 to 4 times with the butter and Crisco until the flour and fat are the sizes of peas. Slowly drizzl in the water, pulsing 4–5 times to fully integrate.

3.Turn the dough out onto a flat surface & roll it into a ball. Wrap the ball with plastic wrap after flattenin; it into a disc. Refrigerate it for a minimum 1 hour before serving.

4.Roll out the dough into a 10-inch pie pan-sized disc. Return back to the refrigerator. To make the fillin; combine flour, sugar, and salt in a small bowl. Using a whisk, combine the ingredients.

5.Whisk the eggs in a medium mixing dish until well combined, then add the flour mixture & whisk t incorporate. Whisk together the butter, lemon juice, and zest. Whisk in the buttermilk thoroughly. Whisk i the vanilla extract thoroughly.

6.Fill the cooled pie shell with the filling. Place on the grill & bake for 45 mins, or until the filling is set a well as the center no longer jiggles. Before serving, let it cool & chill in the refrigerator. Cut into slices an serve. Enjoy!

BACON BOURBON BROWNIES

Prep T: 15 mins /**Cook T**: 20 mins /**Serves**: 16
Ingredients:
- 1/4 cup of bourbon
- 1 tablespoon of Hickory Honey Sea salt
- 2 cups of all-purpose flour
- 1 cup of canola oil
- Salt to taste
- 1 cup of brown sugar
- 6 slices of raw bacon
- 6 large eggs
- 3 cups of white sugar
- Caramel sauce
- 2 tablespoons of instant coffee
- 1/2 teaspoon of smoked in
- 1.5 cup cocoa powder
- 2 tablespoons of instant coffee
- 1 cup of powdered sugar
- 4 tablespoons of water

Directions:

1.Start your pellet grill. Set the temp to 400°F after it's started. Mix together the cocoa, instant coffee, powdered sugar, white sugar, and flour in a large-sized mixing dish, add the oil, eggs, and water to the flour mixture & stir until just mixed.

2.Coat the 9 x 13 pan well with cooking spray, drizzle half of the batter inside the pan with caramel. Pour the remaining batter on top, sprinkle with caramel, then top with candied bacon. In a smoker, bake the brownies for about 1 hour, till a knife inserted in the middle comes out clean, leave to cool prior to slicing after removing from the smoker.

CHERRY PIE SPICED

Prep T: 60 mins /**Cook T**: 20 mins /**Serves**: 6 to 8

Ingredients:

- 1 pound of sweet dark cherries frozen
- 1/2 teaspoon of ground cinnamon
- Juice and zest of 1 lemon
- 1 teaspoon of Hickory Honey Sea salt
- 1 teaspoon of vanilla extract
- 1/2 teaspoon of ground cloves
- 1 cup of granulated sugar
- 1 teaspoon of water whisked with egg (1 egg)
- 1/2 cup of corn-starch
- 2 store-bought prepared pie crust

Directions:

1.Combine the thawed cherries and juices, sugar, lemon zest, corn-starch, vanilla extract, lemon juice cinnamon, clove, & Hickory Honey Sea Salt in a large-sized mixing dish. Allow for 30 minutes of resting time.

2.Spread out 1 of the prepared pie crusts to fit a 9-inch pie tin on a floured work surface. Refrigerate after filling with cherry pie filling. Roll out 2nd pie crust, coat the top of the first using the egg mixture, cover with the second pie crust, pinch the edge using a fork, and refrigerate.

3.Alternatively, split the second pie crust into ribbons and make a lattice pattern with the egg mixture connecting the pieces. Refrigerate the pie for around 15 to 30 minutes, or till the dough is completely cool and hard. Brush the leftover egg mixture over the top of the pie.

4.Preheat your pellet grill to 350°F and cook the pie crust for around 45 minutes to 1 hour, or till brown and hard and the filling is bubbling. Remove off the grill and cool for at least 4 hours at room temperature to solidify the filling, and serve & enjoy!

VEGAN PUMPKIN APPLE MUFFINS GLUTEN-FEE

Prep T: 15 mins /**Cook T**: 20 mins /**Serves**: 12

Ingredients:

- 2 tablespoons of avocado oil
- 1/2 cup of brown sugar
- 1/3 cups of gluten-free oats and more for topping
- 1/4 teaspoon of salt
- 1/2 teaspoon of baking soda
- 1.5 cups of all-purpose gluten flour
- 2 peel core, & dice Granny smith apple
- 1 teaspoon of vanilla extract
- 1 cup of almond milk
- 1 teaspoon of ground cinnamon
- 3/4 cup of pumpkin puree
- 1 batch of flax egg (1 tablespoon of flaxseed meal, 2.5 tablespoons of water)
- 1 tablespoon of vegan butter
- 1 teaspoon of baking powder

Directions:

1. Preheat your pellet grill to 350°F, in a large-sized mixing bowl, prepare the flax egg and set it aside. In a heated pan, melt vegan butter, then stir apples & cinnamon to taste. Cook until tender (3-4 minutes).

2. In the same dish as the flax egg, combine the pumpkin puree, avocado oil, brown sugar, almond milk, and vanilla essence.

3. In a sifter, combine the flour, baking powder, salt, cinnamon, and baking soda. Sift your dry ingredients into the mixing bowl slowly. As you gently add the mixture, stir to incorporate it, stir in the apples & oats until everything is well mixed.

4. Spoon the muffin batter equally into each tray or liner, then top with more oats. Bake for around 25-30 minutes on your grill, or till the toothpick inserted in the middle comes out clean. 12 minutes into the cooking time, rotate the pan.

SKILLET CHEESECAKE BROWNIE

Prep T: 10 mins /**Cook T**: 20 mins /**Serves**: 2

Ingredients:

- 2 eggs
- 1/2 cup of Sugar
- 1 box of brownie mix
- 1/2 cup of oil
- 1 teaspoon of vanilla
- 1 package of cream cheese
- 1 can of blueberry pie filling

Directions:

1. Mix up all of the brownie ingredients. Cream together cream cheese, egg, Sugar, and vanilla in a separate dish until smooth.

2. Brownie batter should be poured into greased skillets. Layer with cheesecake & cherry pie filling, blending with a knife to get the marbled effect. Preheat your Grill to 350°F and bake for 30 minutes. Allow it cool for around 10 minutes before serving.

CONCLUSION

For many individuals, grilling has remained a source of pleasure. Nothing beats sitting outside on your balcony or patio watching burgers and hot dogs sizzle when summer arrives (or whatever you like to cook). Pit Boss grill is one of the best invasions in recent times. Pellet grills can be used in a variety of ways as they are versatile. You can barbeque, grill, smoke, roast, or even braise or bake in a pellet grill. Finally, it is reliable to state that purchasing a pellet grill or smoker will not leave you dissatisfied. It's simple to use, and you'll be able to make nearly anything with it. The nicest part regarding the pallets is that they are consistently proportioned and burn evenly, ensuring an even dispersion of heat throughout the food and more efficient cooking. Because the meal is not cooked over an open flame, blackening and burning are greatly reduced. You may choose the temperature at which you wish to cook with ease. Cook on a low heat level for a longer amount of time; for instance, brisket is ideally cooked on a lower heat setting for a longer time. Similarly, a hotter flame for a shorter time is preferable for the veggies.

You'll find great dishes to try in this book. You may be up & cooking at any anytime of the day or night. Whether you are a vegetarian or a meat lover, there is something for you to make & share with your family and friends.

The best part about the book is that it gives you step-by-step instructions on recipes. All sorts of delicious recipes are included in the book, so you will have plenty of options to choose from. All of these will make your experience much more pleasant. Overall, you will not be disappointed by this experience.

THANK YOU

Dear reader, this book has come to an end. I would take this opportunity to thank you for going through this pages together and making it this far.

I'd love to hear your thoughts on what you've read, what you've learned, and if you would recommend it!

IF YOU ENJOYED THE READ, PLEASE FEEL FREE TO LEAVE YOUR PRECIOUS REVIEW ON THE AMAZON PAGE!

Doing this is **very simple** and will allow other readers like you to make the best choice. Consider including a video or photos to your review, making it even more vivid and informative!

Reach the listing now through this BUTTON/QR CODE and share your thoughts!

THANKS IN ADVANCE FOR YOUR VALUABLE FEEDBACK - I CAN'T WAIT TO READ YOUR OPINION!

THANKS IN ADVANCE FOR YOUR VALUABLE FEEDBACK - As a self-publisher it will allow me to improve my writing and reach more and more people!

PIT BOSS
— WOOD PELLET —
GRILL & SMOKER
— COOKBOOK —

EXTRA BONUS !

.

Made in the USA
Monee, IL
26 November 2022

18610869R00057